Wicked London

by Steve Jones

For Lucinda, Caroline, Sarah & Joanne

INTRODUCTION

If you have no interest in the height of Nelson's Column but would like to meet the bearded lady, visit London's brothels and drinking clubs, experience life in the Blitz and witness early nineteenth-century operations, I am sure you will find 'Wicked London' an educational, interesting and entertaining read.

The opening chapters retell some of the Capital's most famous and sensational murders from the turn of the century to the present day. Later chapters go on to describe the grisly, earthy, sometimes humorous and often bizarre side to London's social history.

'Wicked London' was written to supplement 'London . . . The Sinister Side' which has been selling well since 1986. This is the guide to Tragical History Tours Bus Trip To Murder through the East End and South-East London. The book includes chapters on Jack the Ripper, executions, the hangmen of London and prisons. Both books are available from Tragical History Tours whose address and telephone number may be found on page 88.

First published in 1989 by
Tragical History Tours Publications Limited
1 Bromley Lane, Chislehurst, Kent BR7 6LH
Telephone: 857 1545

©Steve Jones, 1989

ISBN 1-870000-01-3

Typeset and printed in Great Britain by:
DESA Ltd.,
Forest Mills, Alfreton Road, Nottingham.

By the same author:

London . . . The Sinister Side.

CONTENTS

THE MILD-MANNERED DOCTOR

1. The doctor took his lover's letters to the grave.

"In this farewell statement to the world, written as I face eternity, I say that Ethel Le Neve has loved me as few women love men, and that her innocence of any crime save that of yielding to the dictates of the heart is absolute. To her I pay this last tribute . . . My last prayer will be that God will protect her and keep her safe from harm, and allow her to join me in eternity . . . Facing my maker, very close to the hour of my death, I give my testimony to the absolute innocence of Ethel Le Neve. She put her trust in me, and what I asked her to do she did never doubting . . . The world knows what happened afterwards, but what it does not know is the agony we both suffered, the frightful torture of two hearts beating one for another, yet divided by the most cruel barriers."

The slight American doctor penned these words in the condemned cell awaiting the result of a petition against the death penalty. He had time to reflect. Who knows what went through his mind in those last few hours? It was his attraction to the opposite sex which had indirectly led to his present problems. After the early death of his first wife and the birth of their son the doctor fell for the charms of a voluptuous

seventeen year old, Kuningude Mackamotzki. Luckily for us she was also known by the more simple name of Cora Turner. She was far from being a simple girl though and soon became the dominant partner in the marriage as the couple travelled the States, the doctor earning a living from various medical jobs with his wife choosing his clothes and his friends. They could have been the couple that so many English post-cards poke fun at. He, slight, bespectacled and dominated; she, loud, brassy and growing to be twice the woman he married. His relations with his wife could be described as similar to those between a male and female spider. It appeared that Cora had some ability as a singer and in 1899 moved to New York to have her voice trained.

They eventully both came to live in England one year later. Little did either of them know then that their names were going to figure so prominently in British legal history.

In the early years the doctor adored her and even paid the management of music halls to allow her to perform. She was not a great hit and worked very rarely her last appearance being undertaken during a strike by the regular artistes. She was hissed off the stage. It was rumoured that when pickets tried to prevent her from singing Marie Lloyd told them to let her pass as she would most likely drive out the customers!

2. Cora Turner became twice the woman he married.

3. *Hilldrop Crescent: Can you spot the laughing Policeman?*

She was to become a flirt in front of her husband, taunting him with the attentions she paid to other men. He continued to buy her jewels and furs he could scarcely afford, she continued to be miserly and petty in small domestic matters though she put on a completely different face to her theatrical friends. Whenever dinner guests left, they guessed that an argument was about to break out behind the heavy door of the couple's residence.

After what the doctor suspected was an affair between his wife and another American he refused to share the same bedroom and from 1904 onwards probably never slept with her again. He was nonetheless not disenchanted with the female sex and was soon attracted to a quiet and modest nineteen year old he worked with. It is hard to imagine a bigger contrast than between Cora the overweight theatrical and domestic failure and the affectionate and doting Ethel Le Neve, twenty-one years his junior. It was in 1906 that they became lovers.

If the doctor and Ethel had eloped we of course would never have heard of them. There was one stumbling block to this strategy however: all his money was in his wife's name. On the nineteenth of January the doctor took possession of enough hyoscine to poison ten people.

What happened over the next few weeks has never been, and never will be, conclusively proved and we must stick to the facts and present them in their chronological order. Cora disappeared from the social scene and her friends were told that she had been called back to the States on business. Indeed the doctor sent a letter to this effect to Cora's theatrical friends who were perhaps a trifle hurt that she had not been to see them personally but in the short term they accepted the story.

If the doctor had been a little more patient and careful in his actions he would not have been in the cell where if the petition were turned down he would be only hours away from the noose. Only three weeks after his wife's supposed return home he escorted Ethel Le Neve to the Music Hall Ladies Benevolent Fund dinner and ball. These were Cora's old friends and they could not have helped but notice Ethel's jewels, though the last time they saw them was on a somewhat plumper figure. One month later the doctor sent a letter to his wife's friends which finished:

"I have just had a cable saying she is dangerously ill with pleuro-pneumonia . . ."

Four days later he sent a telegram;

"Belle died yesterday at 6 o clock. Shall be away a week" .

He promptly disappeared to France for the said amount of time with the now openly flaunted companion Ethel Le Neve. (She had changed the name from Neave as it sounded more romantic). Cora's friends hounded him on his return demanding where they could send wreaths and asking whether she had left any messages. The

4. *Cora was often hissed off the stage.*

5. *The return under arrest to Britain.*

doctor had to think up answers on the spot and it was from this pressure that he made his first mistake, stating that his son from his first marriage had been with her when she died. He even supplied his address. Letters were sent and one of the friends crossed the Atlantic. No one had seen Belle, no one had heard from her, no one had even heard of her. It was time to call in the police.

It was by now June and Ethel Le Neve had moved into Hilldrop Crescent. Inspector Dew was greeted with a rather different story from the small man with rimless glasses. His wife had left him he said, after a quarrel, and he presumed she had gone back to the States. He invented the story of her death to avoid a scandal. The story on first telling seemed quite credible and the Inspector left without any serious suspicions of foul play.

Early the next week the policeman called into the doctor's office and found that he had wound up his business and left. Mistake number two.

The Inspector returned to Scotland Yard and obtained a warrant to search Hilldrop Crescent. On the third day what appeared to be human remains were discovered under some loose bricks in the coal cellar. There was little more than a small sack of scraps but they included some hair dyed the same colour as Cora's, a piece of skin tissue with an identifiable scar and the viscera still charged with poison. The doctor's defence was later to argue that the remains were not Cora's. What they did not know was that a piece of pyjama belonging to the doctor was found buried alongside the human remains.

"MURDER AND MUTILATION" the bill was headed and contained both the photos of the prime suspects and examples of their handwriting. The information was published in all the newspapers. There is little doubt that both bad luck and poor judgement had played equal parts in the doctor's downfall. He and Ethel had crossed over to Belgium in preparation to taking the 'Montrose' across the Atlantic to a new life in the States. He had shaved his beard, started growing a moustache, stopped wearing his glasses though a white mark across the bridge of his nose where they had been was plainly visible. Ethel Le Neve was dressed as a boy and they were to travel as father and son. They hadn't though counted on Captain Kendall who had read about the findings at Hilldrop Crescent and also their descriptions. The Captain's suspicions were aroused when he noticed the two seemed to be on very intimate terms for a father and son.

6. *Ethel le Neve — and hat.*

'The sea captain turned detective and shouted Mr. Robinson, the passenger's alleged name, after him, but the doctor did not respond. He also drew the medical man into conversation about medicine and proved to himself that his passenger was pretty clued up on the subject. With the doctor's son he deliberately threw a coin into his lap noting that the recipient opened his legs to catch it as if wearing a skirt. Any male would have closed his legs in self-defence!

A message was sent back to England over the wireless and Inspector Dew boarded a faster boat and joined the Montrose just off Quebec.

The doctor was summoned to the Captain's cabin, and the Inspector stepped forward.

"Good morning Dr. Crippen. I am Inspector Dew."

"Good morning, Mr Dew"

"You will be arrested for the murder and mutilation of your wife, Cora Crippen, in London on 2 February last"

Crippen did not reply but later in the day uttered the words that were to cost him so dear at his later trial.

"I am not sorry. The anxiety has been too much"

He later asked about Ethel Le Neve and insisted she knew nothing about it.

The jury were only out for twenty-seven minutes. There was only one possible verdict and Crippen was found guilty though he kept on protesting his innocence before being sentenced.

7. Ethel dressed as a boy.

As he awaited the result of the petition he must have been gladdened at least that his lover had been found not guilty in a later trial. He had written to her every day since and was still hopeful of being reprieved. Indeed an elderly, eccentric ex-soldier offered to change places with Crippen saying that it was immoral to hang a doctor.

The governor approached him and as gently as possible broke the news. The petition for reprieve had failed. Crippen collapsed, sobbing and bubbling like a child. When he recovered he wrote a passionate letter to his lover concluding with the sentence: "There will be no time for letters on Wednesday morning."

On 23 November Hawley Harvey Crippen was hanged and buried in eight feet of earth. In his coffin was a photograph of Ethel Le Neve and the last letter she sent him.

Ethel Le Neve later married and died in Dulwich in 1967 at the age of 84.

BEYOND REASONABLE DOUBT?

Frederick Seddon was a mean man. He never tired of penny-pinching or telling anybody who wanted to listen, and quite a number who did not, how he had climbed up the income ladder. Born to parents of modest means he had progressed through property speculation to becoming a highly-paid member of an insurance company. Frederick was never happy unless maximising profits and with the intention of earning a few extra shillings a week he advertised that the top floor of his house was available for rent.

Eliza Barrow was a mean woman. Having inherited £4,000 she was rich by the standards of the year — 1910. She profited from this wealth by dumping herself on relations who she knew would put her up after hints of a mention in her will. It was a blowsy, prematurely-senile Miss Barrow who knocked upon Seddon's door one summer's day. Her family had had enough of her drunken ways and thrown her out.

A fee of twelve shillings a week was determined and Miss Barrow along with her 'adopted' son 9 year old Ernie Grant moved in. Ernie's main role was to act as companion, personal servant and bed-warmer. There were two other members of Eliza's entourage, Mr and Mrs Hooks but these left within the week after a dispute.

A lonely woman with a plump nest-egg and a scheming man with a smooth tongue under one roof was a recipe for disaster, for both would shortly have their lives prematurely terminated not through the four letter word, love, but the five lettered one; greed.

Once Frederick Seddon found out about Miss Barrow's wealth and the fact that she was not getting sufficient return on her investments, he astutely set himself up as her financial adviser and offered a unique deal. In return for Eliza handing over her wealth to him he would give a fixed amount in gold monthly, for the rest of her life, which as we shall see, was not going to be for very much longer. At first both parties seemed pleased with the deal; Seddon speculating in property in Stepney; Barrow hitting the bottle on her adequate monthly income.

It cannot have taken the astute insurance man long to realise that there was one easy way to considerably increase his monthly income; after eight months a Doctor was summoned to the Seddon's house to attend the poorly Eliza Barrow. She appeared to be suffering from gastritis and asthma, accentuated by her heavy drinking. Eliza took to her bed and was treated for 'summer sickness'. On the fourteenth of September 1911 a certificate giving the cause of death as epidemic diarrhoea was signed by a Doctor Sworn. Ironically Seddon's meanness was to cost him his life. If he had had the body cremated there would have been no evidence against him at his later trial. As it was he had Miss Barrow buried as cheaply as possible and even beat the undertaker down from £4 to £3.7s.6d.

Not surprisingly Eliza's relations, who had not wanted to know her when alive, became very interested and suspicious about her death. They had not been informed of the burial and there were a lot of unanswered questions. Why was a woman of means buried in a public cemetery when there was a family vault in Highgate Cemetery? What had happened to the cash-box she guarded so jealously? Why should such a mean person sign over her wealth to a man she barely knew?

Miss Barrow's relations took their suspicions to Scotland Yard and the body was exhumed. Doctors Spilsbury and Wilcox found the remains saturated in arsenic. Seddon remained calm under questioning but to the surprise of the police asked:

"Are you arresting my wife?"

Mrs Seddon was arrested and charged with murder along with her husband. The prosecution case was extremely circumstantial but helped by the discovery of old newspaper cuttings in the Seddon's home which described the effects of arsenic in an earlier murder case.

The police were puzzled as to how Seddon supposedly got hold of the poison but presented the theory that it had been extracted from boiled fly-papers and administered by the husband or wife in the food and drink or in the medicines.

The evidence was rather weak, but Seddon sealed his own fate in the witness-box when, at the start of his testimony, all he could speak about were his financial affairs. The jury assumed that, as far as the defendant was concerned, money was more important than human life and that he was capable of murder to supplement his bank balance. His wife was found not guilty through lack of evidence. After being found guilty Seddon made a statement to the court which underlined the flimsiness of the prosecution case and went to the rope protesting his innocence:

"I am surrounded by a set of circumstances from which there seems no way of extricating myself if I am condemned by circumstancial evidence . . . In this way, had Miss Barrow thrown herself out through the bedroom window, I would have been believed to have thrown her out or pushed her out through the window. Had Miss Barrow fallen downstairs the same thing would have applied. When she went to Southend-on-Sea then had she fallen into the sea, Mr. Seddon would have pushed her into the sea."

He ended his speech for the first time betraying emotion. Raising his hand in the air he cried:

"I declare before the Great Architect of the Universe that I am not guilty, my lord."

Maybe this was Seddon's last gamble as the gesture exposed him as a mason, as was the judge. We do not know if any secret signs were exchanged in court but the judge was weeping as he donned the black cap and almost apologetically pronounced the death sentence;

"You and I know we both belong to one Brotherhood, and it will be all the more painful to me to have to say what I am saying. But our Brotherhood does not encourage crime; on the contrary it condemns it. I pray you again to make your peace with the Great Architect of the Universe."

This he set out to do from Pentonville on the 18th March 1912.

On the eve of his wife's departure to the United States some months later a newspaper carried the report that she had seen her husband poison Miss Barrow and that he threatened to kill her too if she mentioned the fact. This story was denied a few days later by Mrs Seddon. When asked why she had made it up in the first place she replied that money had been her only motivation.

Frederick Henry would have been proud of her!

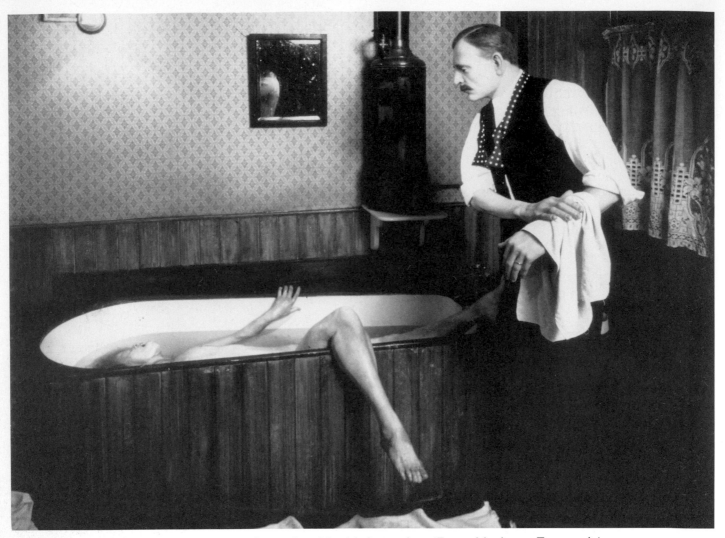

8. *George Smith played the harmonium after his third murder. (From Madame Tussauds)*

THE BRIDES IN THE BATH

George Joseph Smith was a lady-killer by instinct and a killer of ladies by profession. If he had not been so meticulous and thorough in his preparation and dare we say execution of his chosen career he would never have made one of the leading attractions at Madame Tussauds. However original and simple his technique of disposing of his wives once they had outlived their usefulness — usually only long enough to make out their will in his favour — Mr. Smith was to discover that you can fool some of the people some of the time but you can't fool all of the people all of the time.

George Smith spent half of his first sixteen years in a reformatory and was released in 1888 as the Ripper was throwing the East End into a state of panic. As in most reformatories very little was reformed, but there was a great deal of education taking place with the older boys passing tips on crime to their young apprentices. As he was to do more and more frequently in later life the young Smith just disappeared for a few years popping up from time to time to do the odd spell in prison for bicycle theft or larceny.

George blacked his hair and applied pomade. He was a tall, strong man and although not formally educated was certainly no fool. It may have been the influence he had over women in his early life, persuading them to steal for him, that convinced him there was an easier way to make a living than actually going out to work. In the days before poll tax and vehicle licensing offices in Swansea it was fairly easy to travel around the country changing your name as the fancy took you. George Smith became George Love in Leicester where he opened a sweetshop with a newly acquired bride. When he received one of his periodic jail sentences his wife made a sensible decision and fled to Canada.

It is highly unlikely that Smith got any pleasure from the killing he was about to commit. He was no Cassanova but a man desperate for money and it was very likely he had planned his attack before he met Miss Mundy. She was a vulnerable lonely woman and Henry Williams ne Smith, a thirty-five year old picture restorer was placing the wedding ring on her finger just five days after they met. She happened to have some £2,500 in the bank left to her by her father. Try as he might Smith could not get this released as it was carefully guarded by her relations. After he had succeeded in obtaining a small amount he left his wife a note accusing her of giving him venereal disease and indicating that he might return. Unfortunately for the gullible Miss Mundy this is exactly what he did over a year later and the couple were re-united. The day after the couple made out mutual wills George Smith went hunting for a tin bath. The one he bargained for had no taps or fittings and had to be filled and emptied with a bucket. Smith had his murder weapon. He now needed to allay any suspicions of foul play so he took his obedient wife to the doctor twice saying that she had suffered a fainting fit. The third time the doctor sees Bessie Mundy she is clutching a small piece of Castile soap in her right hand, her head is under water and she has apparently drowned in the bath. Smith said that he had gone out to get some herrings for breakfast and when he returned had found his wife dead and sent for the doctor.

Surely any Columbo fan today might be saying, 'Just a minute sir' and gone on to enquire as to why the bereaved husband had not lifted his wife out of the bath, why indeed the bath was on the third floor necessitating walking up two flights of stairs with hot water, and more importantly how anybody could die in a bath that was too small for them. It appears that the coroner and the doctor were more interested in medicine than crime and after burying his wife in a common grave Smith made off with the woman's legacy and returned to another wife saying that he had made some money in Canada. It was not long before this was frittered away and Smith, almost reluctantly, had to turn on the old charm again. This time his victim was to be a stout, merry twenty-six-year-old nurse fourteen years his junior. The nurse, Alice Burnham, took Smith home to meet her parents — who, to say the least — were not over-impressed and the father wrote later to his visitor asking questions about his background. He received the following reply;

"In answer to your application regarding my parentage etc. My Mother was a bushorse, my Father a cab-driver, my sister a rough rider over the Arctic regions and my brothers were all gallant sailors on a steam-roller. This is the only information I can give to those who are not entitled to ask such questions, contained in the letter I received on the 24th inst.

Your despised son-in-law, G. Smith."

The couple were married on the 4th November 1913 and an insurance policy taken out on the young brides life. The modus operandi was the same starting with a visit to the doctor. The family downstairs noticed a large stain of water on the ceiling which enlarged and started running down the walls. Smith arrived in the kitchen of the Blackpool guesthouse stating that he had bought some eggs for breakfast, — a slight change from the 'red herring story' but once again nobody smelt anything fishy as Smith went to his room and shouted down: 'My wife won't speak to me. Fetch Dr Billing in a hurry . . . Oh she is drowned. She is dead.'

Smith went back to the start and collected £650; another 'killing' in Canada.

The third victim was thirty-eight and, like the others, departed the world exactly as she had arrived. The landlady downstairs in Highgate, London heard a splashing sound followed by a large sigh. There then followed ten minutes of harmonium playing. Was Smith beginning to enjoy his work?

The 'accident' was reported in the "News of the World" and that Sunday morning there was one reader who thought he had witnessed the scenario before. Mr Burnham, the father of Smith's second known victim cut out the report and sent it together with a similar account of his daughter's death to the police.

On his way back from the solicitors Smith was met by three men who said they wanted to talk to him about the death of Alice Burnham.

Smith was tried for the murder of Bessie Mundy and not even Marshall Hall could counter the weight of circumstantial evidence. The opening speech for the Crown ended;

"In each case you get the simulated marriage. In each case, all the ready money the woman had is realized. In each case the woman made a will in the prisoner's favour. In each case the property could only be obtained by the woman's death. In each case there were unnecessary visits to a doctor. In each case letters were written the night before the death, in which the prisoner's kindness as a husband was extolled. In each case there were inquiries about a bathroom. In each case the prisoner was the first to discover the death. In each case the prisoner was the person in immediate association with the woman before her death. In each case the bathroom doors were either unfastenable or unfastened. In each case the prisoner pretended to do something which could take him away from the scene where the tragedy had been enacted. In each case there was the immediate disappearance of the prisoner after the inquest."

Faced with this weight of circumstantial evidence against him, Smith sat sullen for the most part but would occasionally interrupt witnesses accusing them of being lunatics or liars. He had enough to shout at as over one hundred witnesses from forty towns were called. Smith was now forty-three but there were still women desperate to get a glimpse of this man whose eyes were the first feature you noticed. They were very bright and piercing but sometimes hardened into a cruel gaze as they did when he told the judge that as he had made up his mind he might as well send him to hang as quickly as possible. The actual baths were brought to the courtroom and a member of the jury tried one out for size. In a police experiment with a female volunteer a man leaning over the bath put one arm under the knees whilst pushing the head down with the other. The volunteer was rendered unconscious by the water rushing up her nose. The experiment almost had catastrophic results.

Whether this was the method used by the strong Smith or whether he just pulled the knees up or pushed the head down we shall never know as after his sentence of death he just lay in his cell making no confession nor showing any penitence.

HANGED FOR IMMORALITY

'Am I right or wrong in saying that this woman is one of the most extraordinary personalities you or I have ever met?'

9. Edith Thompson.

The defence attorney posed the question to the packed courthouse, many of whom had queued since 4am on a cold December morning to be sure of a place in the public gallery. The trial had captured the imagination of the public for several reasons. Edith Thompson who stood in the dock was no ordinary woman. Attractive in a dark rather sultry way she was one of those people whose features reflected every changing mood, no two photographs of her ever appearing the same. She could be romantic and tragically passionate, vivacious and foolishly light-headed. In the winter of 1922 she was on trial for her life and, if convicted of the murder of her husband, could be the first woman to hang for fifteen years. The trial was probably the most sensational of the inter-war years.

Edith earned a good living as a manageress-bookkeeper in the City of London and was now probably earning as much as her husband Percy with whom she had been dissatisfied for a number of years, claiming he used to beat her. She confided in a young man seven years her junior, an attractive seaman by the name of Frederick Bywaters who had become a family 'friend' and had even lived with the Thompsons for six weeks.

On October 5th 1922 in Ilford after returning from the theatre Percy Thompson was savagely attacked from behind and five frenzied stab wounds ended his life. His wife Edith was by his side and a witness later said in court that she had heard a female voice cry out; 'Oh don't don't!'

Edith ran for help and a doctor examining the body by the light of a match declared Percy Thompson dead.

Edith was escorted to the police station in her fur-coat and evening dress and said that she had not seen anybody about at that time and 'did not see a knife or anything.'

She was later to testify that 'a man rushed out at me and knocked me aside . . . When I came to my senses I saw my husband scuffling with somebody down the road.'

With a tip-off from one of Mrs Thompson's neighbours the police went in search of Frederick Bywaters who, when confronted with the crime, denied all the charges. He was arrested, taken to Ilford police station and formally charged with murder. The police had obtained some of the letters Edith had written to Frederick which she told him to destroy, and which were to feature so prominently at the trial. They charged the wife with being a principal at the murder and took her to the same police station. Neither knew the other was being held nor indeed that they were in the same building.

Whether the detectives planned what was to follow or whether it was mere coincidence we shall never know. As Edith was being led past a window in the police station she glanced into a room and saw the young sailor. Not for the first time as we shall note later she was very much shaken and uttered almost involuntarily:

> 'Oh God, why did he do it . . . I didn't want him to do it . . .'

Before long Bywaters was admitting his guilt and in his statement said;

> 'Edith Thompson was not aware of my movements on Tuesday. The reason I fought with Thompson was because he never acted like a man to his wife. He always seemed several degrees lower than a snake. I loved her and could not go on seeing her lead that life . . . I gave him an opportunity of standing up to me as a man but he wouldn't.'

Upon reading the above evidence so far there is the very strong possibility that Edith Thompson was unaware of Bywaters' intentions and any charge of murder against her would be bound to fail. The letters recovered from Bywaters however were to show another side to the rather vain and highly imaginative Edith Thompson. When they were read out in court she sat as if in a trance being constantly fanned by the matron at her side.

10. *Frederick Bywaters at the inquest on Mr. Thompson.*

It appears from the letters that Edith had been trying to kill her husband for some time by adding poison and ground glass to his meals. In her defence it must be said that the pathologist, Sir Bernard Spilsbury, stated that he found traces of neither substance in the contents of the dead man's stomach. In one letter she wrote;

"I'm going to try the glass again occasionally . . . when it's safe."

The case against Edith rested almost entirely on the evidence of her correspondence with Bywaters during his lengthy trips abroad. The most damning was probably the last letter found at her lover's house in Norwood.

"Yes darlint, you are jealous of him but I want you to be. He has the right by law to all you have the right to by nature and love. Yes darlint be jealous so that you will do something desperate."

The jury were out for two and a half hours. The verdicts were announced by the foreman to a hushed courthouse. Bywaters was first. He had walked firmly to his seat and shaken hands with his solicitor. The verdict as expected was 'Guilty'. Edith had been half-carried to her seat by the two wardresses. She did not have long to wait. 'Guilty'.

Edith closed her eyes and seemed on the point of collapse.

Bywaters' final words in court addressed to the jury were;

"I say that the verdict of the jury is wrong. Edith Thompson is not guilty: I am no murderer. I am not an assassin."

Edith's final words were 'Oh God I am not guilty. Oh God I am not guilty.'

They were both sentenced to be hanged.

Both defences decided to appeal, although Bywaters stipulated that nothing should be done in his defence that would prejudice Edith Thompson's appeal.

Freddie's mother writes to the press;

"I am appealing to the hearts of all the mothers of the nation to give me their help in getting a reprieve for my boy. You who have dear boys of your own will I am sure understand the terrible agony I am now suffering, and my great anxiety for his life to be spared. His father gave his life for you and yours, don't let them take my boy from me. From a brokenhearted mother.

Lillian Bywaters."

Along with the Daily Sketch appeal this led to the largest petition ever to be signed in Britain. Bywaters meanwhile was playing draughts and talking about his travels with the prison warders. He showed a keen interest in the football results.

It took just five minutes to dismiss his official appeal on every ground. Freddy glanced at his mother but did not say a word. He wrote to Edith but the letter was not received. He wrote to the Home Secretary protesting Edith's innocence but the letter was not acted upon. Bywaters refused to believe his lover would die. On one of his mother's last visits he is crying. He keeps stating;

'I cannot believe they will hang her.'

He writes again about Edith;

"We will soon be together, and what was not to be on this sordid planet, the land of cowards and curs, will be in another world."

On his last day on this Earth at the age of just twenty years he is dressed in the navy blue suit he had been wearing at the time of his arrest. He is housed in a cell very near to where Crippen lay buried along with his lovers letters. After a breakfast of boiled fish, bread, butter and tea he goes to chapel. He almost rushes to the gallows taking it all in before the white cap condemns him to eternal darkness after a drop of 7'4".

Edith does not wish to be put under public scrutiny again and elects not to attend her appeal, though she was optimistic as to its outcome.

News of the failure of her appeal is broken later that same day by the governor. The execution is scheduled for the 9th January 1923. On Christmas day 1922 Edith Thompson is twenty nine years old. She just nibbles at her chicken before crying out 'What a Christmas' and flying into a fit of hysteria before being sedated. When she comes around she keeps asking 'Why, oh why am I here?' Despite her eating very little Edith's weight increases by over a stone in one month. She was weighed up to three times in one day although she probably did not know this was to help the hangman's calculations.

11. *The young sailor made the mistake of keeping Ediths love letters.*

12. October 1922. Bywaters at the Ilford Station under arrest.

13. December 1922. Mrs. Bywater arriving at the Law Courts to appeal for her sons life.

14. *Bywaters facing the charge of murder.*

Upon contact with the cold air and drizzle Edith began to moan and the white cap is pulled over her face. The figure can hardly support itself and collapses as the hangman kicks the lever. Edith Thompson falls six feet and ten inches. There is a smell of urine and faeces and Mrs Thompson begins haemorrhaging from between the legs. She is left to hang as it is possible that her heart might continue beating for up to thirty minutes.

Rumours begin to circulate that Edith Thompson's insides fell out, and rumours even spread that she was pregnant. The Doctor fails to fill in any details of the internal examination though a great deal of his form was set aside for this information. Special leather underwear became obligatory for the nine women hanged after Edith. Her underwear was washed and her dress burned as the body was prepared for the last visitors. The family arrived and permission was granted to kiss Edith on the forehead. The coffin is covered with lime and Edith laid to rest in the prison's tiny graveyard for nearly fifty years before being moved.

It seemed that Edith Thompson had been hanged for immorality.

The executioner was later to commit suicide and the prison governor and chaplain retired from their posts — the latter devoting the rest of his life to speaking against the death penalty. The Home Office files were marked not to be opened for 100 years.

There was to be no reprieve on the eve of the hanging. Edith becomes hysterical, crying out that she 'never did it' and being sedated with a combination of drugs she enquires as to whether she might write to Freddy. The request is refused. The carpenters erect a wooden screen to protect Mrs Thompson's privacy on her last journey. Edith writes a final letter to her parents whose contents are unknown but it has been confirmed that she made no confession. For her last visit Edith had to be dressed and supported. She merely stares and replies either 'yes' or 'no'. She is suffering with a headache because of the drugs. She sleeps from midnight to 3.15am on her last morning and wakes crying out for Freddy. She is given a cup of tea and later dressed in her silk slip and underclothes. Above these she wears her mourning costume. Her hair is tied back, she does not eat the toast or apple offered for breakfast. At 8.15am one thirty second of a grain of strychnine is administered. More drugs are needed to calm her. She has changed physically beyond all recognition. The hangman and his assistant enter and as her hands are pinnioned behind her back and both skirt and ankles tied one of them mutters;

"Don't worry mate, it'll soon be over."

Edith Thompson is carried like a carcass of meat to the brick shed where nine men and one woman were assembled to witness a most horrific hanging which was to radically alter many of their lives.

15. *Edith Thompson — What secrets lie in the Home Office report?*

The outrage against the hanging of Edith Thompson possibly influenced the sentencing of judges in the following years. There was a murder in Wimbledon just before the Second World War which had many features in common with the Thompson/Bywaters case but is little known today as the sentences were somewhat less terminal.

The murdered man was once again named Percy whose wife Georgina at 38 was twenty years younger than himself. Percy Casserley was an alcoholic and by the year 1938 was consuming one and a half bottles of whisky a day and was allegedly abusing his wife. Money was no problem. He being the managing director of one of London's largest breweries, Casserley's salary was a small fortune for those times.

Georgina took as her lover the foreman at a local building site, Edward Chaplin, who was much closer to her own age, and whilst Percy was in a nursing home, Georgina became pregnant. Both Georgina and Edward wanted to keep the baby and Percy's wife wrote to him at the nursing home asking for a divorce. This was curtly refused in a brief note which read 'Do you think I am such a fool as to give you up for someone else?'

On the day following Percy's discharge from hospital an indignant Chaplin made his way to the family home. He was concerned about the safety of his new love and their unborn child. Ted met Georgina as she was on her way to buy a bottle of whisky for her dipsomaniacal husband who had ignored all hospital warnings. Georgina was afraid to approach her husband and Ted sent her up to her bedroom saying:

"I'll have it out with him."

Instead of the coveted bottle of whisky Percy Casserley was confronted in his own house by the man who had made his wife pregnant.

Percy was outraged by the intruder and, like a character in an early detective novel, made for his revolver hidden in the bureau. Ted Chaplin anticipated the move and after a ferocious struggle the gun went off, resulting in a superficial wound on the back of Casserley's neck. This wound enraged the older man who grabbed hold of his attacker by what was to be termed in court "a part of his anatomy" which as any man will testify, can be very painful in the wrong hands. Ted, in great pain, grabbed a large torch and hit his lover's husband over the head three times. This had the desired effect and free from the older man's grip they fell to the ground. Chaplin later described his drunken opponent as being like "a mad bull". The gun fired a second time and the bull was tamed, shot in the head, just in front of the left ear.

Wiping the gun and picking up the box of cartridges Chaplin made his way upstairs to the terrified Georgina. They made a rather feeble plan which was supposed to suggest that Percy had been shot by an intruder. We shall never know whether Percy heard these plans as at the time he was still alive lying in a pool of blood. When the police arrived, however, Percy Arthur Casserley, at the age of 58 had had his last drink.

It did not take the police long to piece the story together and on the day when Percy was being buried Chaplin was being charged with his homicide. Three days later Georgina was arrested and charged with being an accessory after the murder. Adultery was still very much frowned upon and despite her pregnancy Mrs Casserley was given a harsh time in Holloway prison, having to scrub the floors and being refused a bath before being released on bail.

The evidence at the trial did not seem to match Ted Chaplin's version of the events. Despite the supposed hard fight between the two men over seventeen bruises were found on the deceased whereas not a single mark was found on the accused. After a lot more damaging evidence the prosecution summed up their case "I suggest that the accused made up his side of the story of the struggle to fit the facts."

In his summing up the judge advised the jury;

"What you have to decide is, did Chaplin unlawfully cause the death of Mr Casserley, and if he did, did he do it with the intention of causing him grievous injury?"

He continued that should they agree that Mr Casserley had been shot: "In the heat of passion in the course of a quarrel so serious that the accused lost complete control of himself they must convict of manslaughter and not murder." Mrs Casserley fainted when she heard the verdict — Not guilty of murder, guilty of manslaughter.

A few minutes later she was put in the dock herself. The judge had been incensed at the sympathetic publicity the conspirator after the event had been receiving and he warned her;

"The less said about you and your part in this case the better. I am not going to treat you with leniency because I think there is nothing particular in your condition that calls for it. Your case has aroused the most ridiculous nonsense. A great many people have treated you as if you were some sort of heroine. You were a participant in a vulgar and sordid intrigue. Now please go!"

Whereas Thompson and Bywaters were both hanged Mrs. Casserley was sentenced to eleven days in prison and Edward Chaplin to twelve years. With remission he came out after eight to find Georgina waiting for him at the prison gates. They went straight to the registry office to become Mr and Mrs Chaplin.

THE ACID-BATH MURDERER

16. *The ex-choir boy who did a crossword throughout his murder trial.*

John's parents, members of the Plymouth Brethren religious sect, segregated him from other children lest he might pick up bad habits. He learnt to recite whole passages from the Bible and sang solo in the Wakefield Grammar School Choir. He would turn the pages for the organist and was the star pupil in both Religious Studies and Chemistry. His handwriting was held up as an example for all to copy and his school career probably peaked when he won the prize for Divinity.

He left school rather small for his age showing little interest in girls and rarely smoked or drank. John's father was pleased his son was studying insurance and hire-purchase law whilst still attending Mass on Sundays. The 'perfect' son also showed a keen interest in the law in general and read a great deal in his spare time.

By the age of thirty-nine John Haigh had apparently lost all interest in legal matters as he sat passively in the courtroom struggling over the clues of a crossword puzzle. He seemed to show little interest in the trial in process, even though it was his own! He looked up occasionally to borrow an eraser to correct one of his answers.

The court house was heaving with hundreds outside eager to catch a glimpse of the accused, who, on his own admission, had murdered nine people and disposed of their bodies in a unique and gruesome manner. In his first written statement to the police he described his modus operandi when he recounted the murder of his last victim.

"I shot her in the back of the head . . . Then I went out to the car and fetched in a drinking glass and made an incision, I think with a penknife, in the side of the throat and collected a glass of blood which I then drank. Following that I removed the coat she was wearing, a persian lamb, and the jewellery, rings, necklace, ear-rings and crucifix, and put her in a forty-five gallon tank. I then filled up the tank with sulphuric acid by means of a stirrup pump from a carboy. I then left it to react. I should have said that in between putting her in the tank and pumping in the acid I went round to the Ancient Priors for a cup of tea."

There is considerable doubt as to the veracity of the consumption of blood, most experts thinking this was fabricated by the defendant to support his plea of diminished responsibility. The rest of the story was never doubted. John George Haigh will always be better known as the "Acid Bath Murderer."

What had become of the gifted school-boy? In all honesty he had only appeared as such to his parents and the odd school-teacher. From his early years he was a bully to those younger and smaller than himself. He took a delight in torturing insects and animals and became a very cunning and skillful liar.

Leaving school without passing his final exams he was always to be found immaculately turned out and was rarely seen without kid-gloves, even in summer. His first love in life was motor cars which he financed from suspect hire purchase agreements and forgery. He married at the age of twenty five but his wife with good foresight left him during his first prison sentence. In the late thirties and early forties he was in and out of prison where he managed to procure some acid and started doing experiments on mice.

Haigh was released towards the end of the war, determined never to return. Nothing and nobody was going to stand in the way of his living the affluent kind of life style to which he thought himself entitled.

Money flowed through Haigh's extraordinarily large hands like water most of it being lost gambling or buying cars. Towards the latter end of 1944 Haigh, living in South Kensington, committed his first murder in a basement in Gloucester Road. John McSwann, Haigh's business partner, was hit from behind with a cosh and his body immersed in acid. The sludge that remained was disposed of down a manhole in the basement. McSwann was the first victim of nine over a five year period, the process varying little.

The Acid Bath Murderer was caught after a friend of the last victim went to the police to report her missing. Haigh had proposed a business venture and brash as ever himself went to the police station to make a statement. The police became suspicious after finding inconsistencies in his story. Haigh saw that the net was closing in but mistakenly thought that if there was no body he could not be prosecuted.

In fact there were parts of the last body remaining. To be precise there were twenty eight pounds of melted body fat, part of a left foot, three gallstones and eighteen fragments of human bone eroded by acid. The body was positively identified through a set of lower and upper dentures.

Haigh saw the game was up and played his last gamble, the one that more than any other sent him to the gallows. During interrogation he asked the police:

"Tell me frankly, what are the chances of anybody being released from Broadmoor?"

Haigh was preparing his plea of diminished responsibility. He had always been a lousy gambler.

The jury deliberated for less that fifteen minutes.

"Have you anything to say why sentence of death should not be passed on you?" The judge asked showing no emotion.

"Nothing at all" was the reply as Haigh smiled and shrugged his shoulders.

Haigh's last days were spent playing chess with his prison officers. He smoked the alloted ten cigarettes a day but did not touch the beer ration. He had never lost his appetite and ate heartily, writing to his mother every day. John Haigh's life seemed to have come full circle as he read long passages from the Bible before his execution. He showed uncommon interest in the waxwork model which would be exhibited in the Chamber of Horrors at Madame Tussauds.

At 9am on the tenth of August 1949 John George Haigh was hanged, probably the most callous, cold-blooded and vain murderer the capital had housed. The outcry against capital punishment was noticeable by its absence!

17. Haigh took great interest in his wax-work to be exhibited in the Chamber of Horrors. (From Madame Tussauds).

THE AIRMAN TAKES HIS FINAL FLIGHT

18. Neville Heath — sadistic lady killer. (From Madame Tussauds).

'Come on, boys, let's be going'. Neville Heath played the well-educated gent to the last as he hurried the executioner to the gallows. What turned a tall, blond, intelligent man of twenty-nine into a sadistic sex killer?

After a series of enlistings and court-martials in different air-forces around the world the well-spoken Neville Heath returned, via a marriage in South Africa, to an England still trying to rebuild after six years fighting. Posing as 'Lord Dudley' in June 1946 the imposter took a double room at Notting Hill Gate Hotel and awarded himself the rank of Lieutenant-colonel. In a few hours he had returned with an attractive woman in her early thirties who it was later discovered enjoyed violent sex and had masochistic tendencies. The following morning finding the bedroom locked and with no reply to her knocking the chambermaid asked the assistant manageress for advice. They entered the room with a master key at 2pm and drew back the curtains. There was a man's handkerchief on one of the beds, not so unusual you might think, but for the fact that it bound together the ankles of the otherwise naked body of the female guest. There were marks on both wrists and the woman's arms had been folded behind her. Seventeen deep gashes could be counted and extensive injuries to the vagina were thought to be caused by a steel-tipped whip. All the injuries had been inflicted before death which was due to suffocation. Not one of the hotel guests heard a sound.

Heath made his way to the south coast and wrote a letter to the police stating that he had allowed the victim, Mrs Gardner, to use his room and later returned to find her body. He did not go to the police for fear of being implicated.

In Bournemouth he dated an ex-Wren who was last seen alive accompanying him back to the hotel room. The mutilated body of Doreen Marshall was discovered a few days later. The corpse was once again naked and one nipple had almost been bitten off. The front of the body had been cut several times and once again there were serious injuries to the genitals by some rough instrument. Again, the wrists had been tied.

It appears that Heath wanted to be caught as he walked into Bournemouth police station and was immediately recognised and arrested.

The evidence against him was overwhelming especially as police had found his steel-tipped riding whip. Heath had wanted to plead guilty but when told this might cause distress to his family replied;

"All right, put me down as not guilty, old boy."

It was remarked in court that 'He is a most abnormal person is he not' and nobody would disagree. Almost the only words in his defence came from a psychotherapist who claimed that Heath was not an ordinary sexual pervert but was suffering from moral insanity and at times did not know what he was doing. The witness, who was found dead from a drug-overdose six months later, would have certified him as morally insane.

Heath refused to make an appeal and was hanged in Pentonville Prison on 26th October 1946.

THE TRUTH IS RARELY PURE AND NEVER SIMPLE

"I have disposed of my wife. I put her down the drain."

The detective-constable gazed increduously at the slight young man in front of him at Merthyr Vale Police Station.

"Yes, I know what I am saying. I can't sleep and want to get it off my chest. I will tell you all about it and you can write it down."

19. Timothy Evans — has difficulty separating fact from fantasy.

Timothy Evans had gone into the Welsh police station of his own free will and was offering the first of three statements concerning the disappearance of his attractive wife, Beryl. As the policeman noted down the details he must have been wondering about this semi-literate van driver whose account of his wife's death seemed more and more implausible the longer he listened. Evans, who had difficulty telling fact from fiction, settled down to his task.

The couple were living in the top floor of 10, Rillington Place, North London. Looking around their shabby room it was no surprise that when Beryl became pregnant for the second time, the couple already having a baby girl, Geraldine, she seriously considered having an abortion. The family had financial problems with Timothy's seven pounds a week wage barely being able to meet the rent and hire-purchase payments. As far as Beryl was concerned another baby was out of the question, but in 1949 abortion was still very much a shadowy, back-street industry carried out by men and women with a variety of implements and precious few qualifications. Timothy wanted his wife to have the baby and there were frequent rows between the two. By the time Evans walked into the police station his wife was over three months pregnant. For a man who was supposed to be against his wife losing their child, the following events in Evans's first statement seem rather difficult to believe:

While eating in a transport cafe Evans met a complete stranger and told him about the difficulties he was having with his wife. Just by chance Evans's new 'friend' happened to have the solution to their problems. He went out to his vehicle, returning a few mintues later with a small bottle wrapped in brown paper. He made no charge for the liquid and gave instructions that his wife should take it the next morning before tea. The mystery man then disappeared. Evans and his wife acted upon these instructions and the next evening Timothy returned to their dingy flat to find Beryl's dead body. The following morning he opened the drain outside the front door of his house pushing her corpse down head first. He then added that he managed to get the baby looked after, sold his furniture, and moved down to Merthyr Tydfil where he now sat.

The Welsh police contacted their London counterparts and the drain outside Rillington Place was raised. It had taken far more strength than the slight Evans could have mustered to lift it but the police not surprisingly found no signs of any body.

It was time for Evans to make his second statement and this time he tried to implicate an ex-soldier and policeman who had served his country and lived in the same house on the ground floor. Evans suggested that his neighbour had heard of the couple above's problem and said he could help. Returning home from work the next day the neighbour invited him into a room whose curtains were ominously drawn. Hesitatingly Timothy pulled back the eiderdown and described what he saw; "I could see that she was dead and that she had been bleeding from the mouth and nose and that she had been bleeding from the bottom part."

20. Evans' neighbour whom he accused of murder.

The neighbour had reportedly told him that the abortion had gone wrong and that he would make all arrangements, for disposal of the body and care of the baby. He advised Evans to leave the scene of the crime.

Although there was as yet no body the police were extremely suspicious and went through Rillington Place with a fine toothcomb. On their second search they peeked into a wash-house in the compact back garden which was tended by Evans's neighbour. Beryl's petite body had been wrapped up and folded in half. The baby girl was discovered in the corner, a man's tie knotted tightly around her neck.

The bodies were in a remarkably good state of preservation considering they had been dead three weeks. Both mother and daughter had died from strangulation, the mother with a rope. There was a little ante-mortem bruising around the vagina. Beryl was sixteen weeks pregnant.

When Evans was informed about the discovery of his wife and child and the circumstances of their death he did not seem too surprised. The Welshman made his third statement, this time a full confession and even appeared quite animated as he told his story. Evans confided that the family were slipping deeper into debt and arguing a great deal. On the 8th of November he lost his temper and strangled his wife with a rope, killing the baby two days later. He disclosed that it was a great relief to get it off his chest and said that he felt a lot better already.

Some time later after consulting a solicitor the defendant retracted the statement and reverted to number two, the involvement of the man downstairs.

One of the strange features of the case was that much to the anger of the defence Evans was charged not with the murder of his wife but that of his baby daughter, Geraldine.

The main prosecution witness was the neighbour whom Evans had implicated but the court heard of his commendable public service and the prosecution stated that the neighbour — being in poor health — was physically incapable of murder and had no motive.

Evans appeared as the sole witness for the defence and under cross examination was proved to be a liar. 'Why should anybody believe a word he said?' the judge seemed to imply in his summing up. When Evans was asked why his neighbour should have committed the murder he replied:

"Well, he was home all day."

The jury took just thirty-five minutes to find Evans guilty. The sound of a man sobbing filled the hushed courtroom as the judge pronounced sentence;

"Timothy John Evans, the jury has found you guilty of wilful murder and the sentence of the court upon you is . . ."

The judge went on to impose the dealth penalty.

The trial took place on Friday the thirteenth of January.

Evans ate and slept well in Pentonville Prison and was a well-behaved prisoner, playing cards and in fairly good spirits even after his appeal was turned down. He showed no remorse, and was not angry but seemed resigned and indifferent to his fate. He went to confessional with a priest prior to his execution on the ninth of March 1950 but details of the conversation will never be revealed.

There was no public outcry most people viewing the case as a squalid domestic affair. Why, you may be wondering, has the case become one of the "Great British Trials?" For two reasons: The tears heard in court upon the conviction were not Evans' but those of the chief prosecution witness, John Reginald Halliday Christie, and Timothy Evans was not guilty!

Christie and his wife left the courtoom to the screams of "Murderer, murderer!" emanating from Evans's enraged Mother.

"Don't you dare call my husband a murderer. He is a good man" replied Mrs Christie — not the world's greatest judge of character. There was only one man who knew if there were any skeletons in the cupboard and he was off to his native Yorkshire to get over the ordeal.

21. *John Christie taken to court.*

TEN RILLINGTON PLACE

John Christie had been born fifty-two years earlier and like John Haigh, whose case he followed closely, sang in the choir. He was also a keen gardener! In 1916 he enlisted in the army, serving in France before being injured by a shell blast and blinded for five months. It was at about this time that he lost the ability to speak for three and a half years though this may have been a mental rather than a physical problem.

In 1920 Christie married Ethel Simpson Waddington but appears to have encountered sexual difficulties, and many psychologists believe these problems may have led to his future behaviour. Three years later he left his wife and came to London but over the next few years fell into a life of petty crime and was imprisoned for short terms for stealing postal orders and other goods. His conviction involving violence was for attacking a young lady about the head with a cricket bat. Ethel Christie did not make one of her better decisions in life when she came to the capital to re-join her husband after a nine year separation. In 1938 the couple moved in to the ground floor flat at number ten Rillington Place. The next year, with the outbreak of war, Christie took up full time duties as a special constable in the War Reserve which he continued until December 1943.

After Evans's conviction and hanging the Christies continued to live in the same flat. The house was put up for sale and bought by a Jamaican landlord who moved some of his country people into the recently vacated upstairs flat. Christie was very disturbed by these events and under no circumstances would the nervous Yorkshireman allow the new residents to work in the garden. The trusting Mrs Christie was last seen alive on 12th December 1952. Soon after this date Christie contacted the same furniture dealer as had Evans and sold most of his possessions, though he did not move out straight away. He stayed on in the cold house, sleeping on an old mattress with a few dirty blankets. The day came when (probably for financial reasons) Christie decided to move. The Jamaicans upstairs were given permission to use the kitchen in the flat and whilst fixing up a bracket for the wireless the tenant discovered a hollow wall. Tearing back the wallpaper he found a small gap. Looking through this hole the would-be decorator was faced with a grisly sight; sat in the rubble was the corpse of a naked woman.

The police were immediately summoned and with the removal of the artificial wall were faced with a corpse whose clothes had been forced up but whose head was hanging down; from the nose a bloody fluid had taken on a form of mould. Behind the first body lay a second and then a third, each squatting on the head of the other. The fourth body, this time under the floorboards, was that of Mrs Christie, whose famous line, 'my husband is a good man' must go down in any black book of quotations.

Because of the cold in the rooms the bodies had been fairly well preserved. The three women — all in their mid twenties — were 'not without sexual experience'. There were no knickers on any of the bodies and living spermatozoa were found in all three victims, intercourse having taken place at the time of, or after, death. The freshest body was about four weeks old and the other two between eight and eleven weeks. Like Mrs Evans they had all been strangled; there was strong evidence to suggest their having first been gassed. The third body to be found i.e. the first murdered was six months pregnant at the time. The first two had cloth in the position of a diaper placed between their legs.

No spermatozoa were found in Ethel Christie's body though she too had a piece of cloth in the same position. She had been strangled before the others and had been dead anything between twelve and fifteen weeks. Whilst searching the premises the police found a tobacco tin containing four different sets of pubic hair, it later being established that these belonged to none of the victims so far discovered. The search switched to the garden where several bones, both human and animal, were discovered. A human thigh bone had even been driven into the earth as the prop for a fence. Human hair still held by a Kirby grip was discovered along with burned bones and teeth. Two female skeletons were eventually assembled though the skull of one was missing. The remains dated back about ten years to 1943 or 1944. The murder of Mrs Evans and baby Geraldine were evidently not the first perpetrated at Ten Rillington Place.

Christie's photo was plastered all over the national press and a dishevelled figure was approached by a policeman on the banks of the Thames. Once he responded to the request to take off his hat the policeman knew he had his man. Furthermore Christie's wallet contained a cutting about Timothy Evans. When told about his wife he burst into tears and put forward his explanation about her death. We must be very careful when listening to any statements from Christie as he was without doubt a very clever liar as he had proved in court three years earlier. Whereas Evans told lies because of his low I.Q. and suggestible nature, Christie was cunning and ruthless. 'She woke me up. I couldn't stand it any longer. I couldn't bear to see her suffer. You know what I did.'

He went on to describe how he had tied a stocking round his wife's neck to help her to sleep. He left the body for two or three days as he did not know what to do. The body was eventually secreted under the floorboards.

Christie's further confessions did not ring true. He stated that the first victim accosted him in the street asking for money. She somehow got into the house and was about to attack him with a frying pan, when in self-defence, he hit her against a deck-chair. ''I must have gone haywire'', Christie added before admitting to strangling the young woman.

At first Christie denied murdering Mrs Evans but later changed his mind though remaining adamant to his dying day that he did not murder the baby. Christie said that the pubic hairs in the tobacco box were from the young ladies in the alcove, but this proved not to be the case. He also said that one clump had come from Mrs Evans. Beryl had been buried with her baby in the same coffin and the bodies were exhumed. Both being fairly well preserved it was proved that Christie had been lying again.

According to Christie he had murdered his first victim whilst having intercourse during the war. He was supposed to have received a telegram from his wife who said she was coming home that evening: Christie panicked and disposed of the body in the garden.

Of the second he noted, ''I believe I had intercourse with her at the time I strangled her.''

As for the three who perished after his wife, they were all supposed to have been made drowsy by gas emanating from under the deck chair, Christie finishing them off with his bare hands before getting down to his sexual perversions. He never satisfactorily explained how he himself was not affected by the gas.

On remand Christie kept looking at a photo of himself and comparing himself with the acid bath murderer in his cell. He slept well.

There could only have been one defence and in his opening speech defence counsel argued:

''My submission is that the evidence is such that there is no other conclusion to be found than that he is as mad as a March hare when he kills people.''

The jury did not agree and after the four day trial found Christie guilty of murder. He was sentenced to hang and did not appeal. It is unlikely we shall ever know the truth about the murder of baby Geraldine, as throughout his whispered statement in court Christie never admitted his guilt as to this crime.

Timothy Evans was later cleared of his conviction.

22. *Christie with his wife — one of his six murder victims.*

"LET HIM HAVE IT, CHRIS"

23. *Christopher Craig — too young to hang.*

Christopher Craig held a grudge against the police. His brother had been sent down for twelve years, and Christopher had been rather moody and depressed since leaving school. Now a sixteen year old in the Winter of 1952, he had set his rather limited sights on a life of crime. After the war there were many guns still in private hands and during his school career Craig claimed to have swopped arms anything up to fifty times. He certainly did not pay much attention to his studies being barely literate with limited writing ability, his sisters reading to him in the evenings. Christopher, who liked to dress in a long coat with a trilby hat, was a frustrated adolescent who hated the world. A bizarre and still unexplained series of

events was to lead to the death of two men and the discussion of Craig's case in the House of Commons.

Derek Bentley at nineteen was chronologically three years Craig's senior though having the mental age of a ten to eleven year old and an I.Q. of 66. He could not even spell his own christian name. To add to his problems he suffered from epilepsy and after failing to hold down jobs as a furniture remover, dustman and roadsweeper was found to be unfit for military service. The gods had not dealt Derek a very strong hand of cards. As can be imagined he was not the capital's most successful thief and had spent two years in corrective training, though he had no record of violence.

Derek was watching television on the evening of the 2nd November when Craig called. After combing his wavy fair hair and inspecting his drainpipe trousers he bade his parents farewell and joined Craig on the short journey from South London to Croydon. He left the organisation to the younger man.

Trilbys pulled down and collars turned up as in American gangster movies, the two must have looked rather pathetic in their own make believe world as they scoured Croydon looking for some premises to break into. Derek was later to claim that he did not know that Christopher had a gun, a .455 Eley revolver with a sawn-off barrel, his father having taught him to shoot as a boy. Derek for his part carried a sheath knife and a fearsome knuckleduster especially rendered more dangerous by Craig.

The young men decided upon a course of action and climbed twenty-two feet up some drainpipes to the top of a building. They were spotted by a nine-year-old whose father went to a call box to alert the local police — their headquarters being just a stone's throw away. What happened over the next half-hour has never been conclusively proved. Both who said and who did what have been confused by the darkness, Derek Bentley's inability to express himself clearly, the firing of several bullets in the murky light and the tragic death of a policeman. What is generally accepted to have happened is as follows:

A police van arrived followed a few minutes later by a police car. The two miscreants on the roof were alerted as to their presence by the light of torches and the sound of voices below. Detective-Constable Fairfax was in plain clothes as he clambered up to the roof. This as far as he knew was just another routine case as he walked towards the boys hiding behind a chimney stack. He did not have a torch and the visibility was poor.

"I am a police officer. Come out from behind that stack"

Unbeknown to the policeman Craig's hand was probably on the trigger as he replied.

"If you want us, fucking well come and get us" .

Fairfax rushes the stack, manages to grab hold of Bentley and tries to seize Craig with the other hand but he is too quick and slides away.

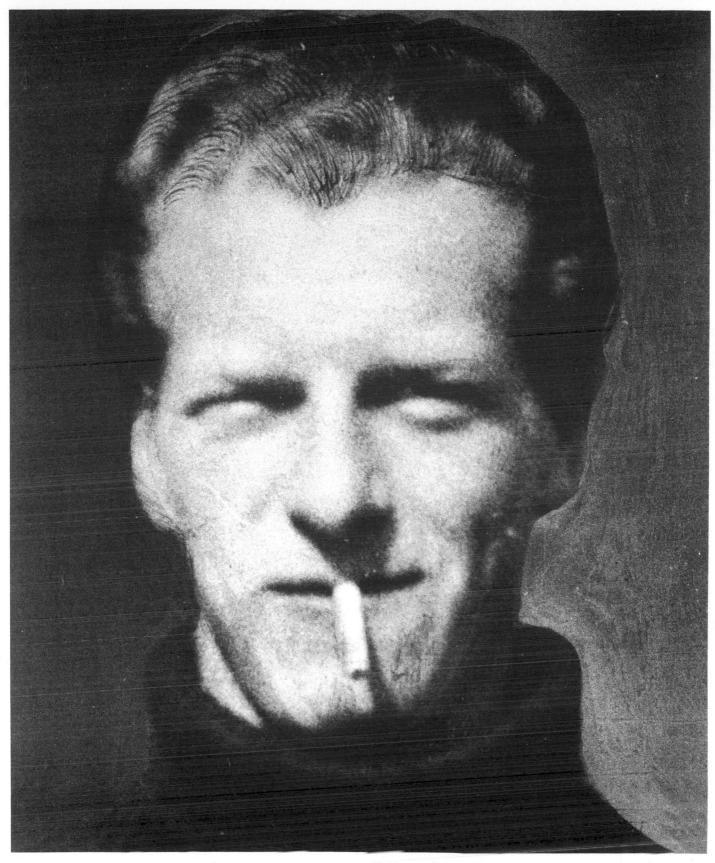

24. *Derek Bentley — the judge ignored the jury's recommendation to mercy.*

A second policeman arrives on the scene and Fairfax shouts out that he has hold of one of the intruders. Fairfax, at the subsequent trial, then stated that Bentley broke away and shouted out five of the most famous words in post war criminal history.

"Let him have it, Chris." To his dying day Bentley denies ever uttering these words. A shot rings out and Fairfax is hit in the right shoulder though he manages to recapture Bentley, knocking him to the ground with his fist.

Another bullet is discharged and Fairfax, using Bentley as a shield, tries to get him downstairs. After kicking a door open another policeman, the unarmed Sidney Miles gains access to the roof. Miles is trying to join Fairfax and Bentley when a bullet catches him in the face and he is fatally wounded, the charge now being murder. The police are still unarmed and throw anything they can get their hands on including a truncheon and a bottle of milk, at the young murderer. Craig the defiant headstrong adolescent shouts;

"You've just given my brother twelve years. Come on you coppers, I'm only sixteen."

Craig is firing wildly at anything on the roof and as Fairfax tries to force Bentley downstairs, the prisoner, probably in self-defence is shouting;

"They're taking me down now Chris."

Bentley is safely removed and Fairfax returns to the roof though this time he is armed. He hears Craig's gun click and can just make out what the young man intends to be his last words;

"Give my love to Pam."

He dives headfirst off the roof into the glasshouse below. When the police reach him he is still conscious, and defiant to the last he gasps;

"I wish I was fucking dead. I hope I've killed the fucking lot."

He is taken to hospital with a fractured spine, breast bone and left wrist.

Over the next few weeks Craig becomes one of the star attractions in the 'outraged' popular press. Parents had fought the second world war for these children and were rewarded with an ungrateful bunch of young hoodlums and anti-social adolescents. Craig's rather feeble 'gangland' activities were blown up out of all proportion and financial incentives were made to his family for any information about the murderer they could provide. Derek Bentley was for the most part forgotten.

As can be imagined Craig had little defence though his lawyer did suggest manslaughter would be a more appropriate charge. The case against Bentley was not helped by the defendant's poor showing in the witness box; he was like putty in the hands of one of the country's most skillful prosecutors. The jury were out for seventy-five minutes.

"How do you find Christopher Craig, guilty or not guilty of murder?"

"Guilty"

How do you find Derek William Bentley, guilty or not guilty of murder?"

"Guilty, with a recommendation to mercy."

The judge, donning his black cap addressed Bentley first;

"Derek William Bentley, you are nineteen years of age. It is my duty to pass upon you the only sentence which the law can pass for the crime of willful murder. The sentence of the court upon you is that you be taken from this place to a lawful prison, and thence to a place of execution, and there you suffer death by hanging, and that your body be buried within the precincts of the prison in which you shall have been last confined before your execution. And may the Lord have mercy upon your soul"

It is unsure whether Bentley knew what was happening before the command of "take him down" was acted upon.

Craig being too young for the death sentence was ordered to be detained at Her Majesty's pleasure after being described as "one of the most dangerous young criminals who ever stood in the dock."

The press continued to show some interest in Craig's case, assuming that the recommendation for mercy would prevent the overlooked figure of Derek Bentley from hanging. As it turned out Craig was to serve about ten years before being released. His role in the drama was effectively over.

Hopes were high when Bentley's appeal came up; he had been in police custody when the shot had been fired and the jury had recommended mercy. The case was dismissed within one hour. It seemed Bentley's life was of little significance. It was only then that the fickle British Press, recently screaming for revenge, began to take an interest in this boy in a man's body who faced the prospect of hanging for murder without having even fired a shot. Michael Foot, the future leader of the Labour Party, attacked the judge in the Herald. Nonetheless the day for execution was set for January the twenty-eighth two weeks after the final appeal. There was still the possibility of a reprieve from the Home Secretary and it was with this end in mind that the condemned man's parents launched a last-ditch campaign. Over one hundred thousand signatures for a reprieve were collected and the newspapers and government offices flooded with the public's pleas for mercy. Meanwhile Derek seemed to be bearing up fairly well under the strain. On prison visits he would talk about his pets: two cats; three whippets and the rabbits.

Stickers claiming "Bentley must not die" were circulated and many questions were asked in the House. The Home Secretary looked unlikely to change his mind. On the day before the execution Derek Bentley's parents visited him for what was to be the last time. As they left Derek's final words were "I will see you tomorrow." He dictated his last letter to a sympathetic prison warder where he talked about pets, pies and T.V. sets. His mind jumped from one topic to another adding some advice to his father:

"Oh, Dad, don't let my cycle frames get rusty they might come in handy one day."

There was a large demonstration outside parliament, with the crowd marching to the Home Office, but all was to no avail so they returned to the prison and sang "Abide with me."

On the other side of the wall Derek was led quietly sobbing to the trap.

Although the official executioner was to later to deny it, his last words were reported to be;

"I didn't say it. I didn't tell Chris to shoot that policeman."

'HELL HATH NO FURY'

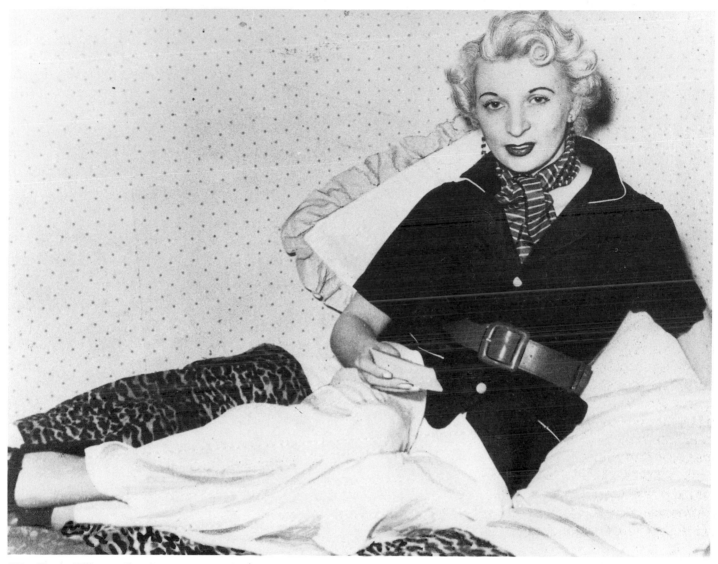

25. Ruth Ellis — the last woman to hang.

"David!" was the only word cried by the platinum blonde as she approached her lover.

Dressed in a grey two-piece with a green sweater she closed in on David Blakely who was vainly searching for his car keys. He knew Ruth well and started to panic as he noticed her chill dertermined eyes. Ruth opcned her handbag and pulled out a heavy Smith and Wesson .38. The two shots were fired in quick succession, the first from a range of just three inches. Blakely, writhing in agony, called the name of his friend. Clive stood motionless until being ordered out of the way by the determined twenty-eight year old club manageress. She advanced coolly on her prey and fired once again. 'Even after the body lay motionless on the pavement Ruth kept shooting until the chamber was empty. Four bullets had hit their intended target and one a woman passer-by though she was not seriously injured.

Ruth made no attempt to escape and apparently unmoved, was driven to Hampstead Police Station. All she would say at first was,

"My name is Mrs Ruth Ellis. I am a model. I am 28 and I live at 44, Egerton Gardens, that's in Kensington."

Later the next morning she told her story;

Ruth was a determined and competent woman who had worked her way up from machine minder in South London to manageress In a night-club. Part of her rise was probably due to good looks and her part-time profession as a high-class prostitute with regular customers.

26. 'It was obvious when I shot him I intended to kill him.'

At her trial it had taken a great deal of persuasion from her defence for Ruth to plead 'not guilty' to the charge of murder. She sat, immaculately turned out, detached and cold as the prosecution asked the question that was to lead to Ruth's hanging:

"Mrs Ellis, when you fired that revolver at close range into the body of David Blakely what did you intend to do?"

"It was obvious that when I shot him I intended to kill him."

With these words, spoken unhesitatingly, Ruth Ellis could only be convicted of murder and not manslaughter.

Ruth smiled towards her friends in the spectators gallery after the pronouncement of the death sentence. There was no appeal and Ruth refused to say anything more about the shooting. She showed no remorse but wrote to Blakely's mother saying;

"I shall die loving your son, and you should feel content that his death has been repaid."

She glanced at the photo of David's grave in her cell before despatching the letter.

Ruth Ellis showed no outward fears of the hangman's noose and even quipped that it would be no more alarming 'than having a tooth out'. On July 13th 1955 with a steady hand Ruth Ellis downed her last tot of brandy and thanked the Holloway staff for their kindness. She stepped into the execution shed — and the history books — as the last woman to be hanged in Britain.

After an unsuccessful marriage to an alcoholic dentist she left when her second baby was born, Ruth already having a child from a wartime romance. Ruth met the charming racing-car enthusiast, David Blakely at her club. Romance blossomed and in 1953 the night-club manageress aborted David's child. It was a very torrid affair with both parties blowing hot and cold and Ruth taking on a second lover, ostensibly to make David jealous. There was another abortion in 1955 though David was not sure whether it was his or not. During one of the happier phases of their relationship the warring couple moved into a one-bedroomed apartment in Kensington in the name of Mr & Mrs Ellis. It soon seemed they could not live with or without each other. After Ruth's ten year old came to share the same bedroom Blakely told friends;

"I want to get away from her."

David Blakely went missing and Ruth guessed that he was having an affair with the attractive nanny of one of their friends. Armed with the gun that she later said had been given to her by a friend three years previously she went looking for him at one of his favourite drinking establishments. At 9pm on Easter Sunday, 1955 she found him.

27. *Ruth and David — the man she shot in cold blood.*

MOTIVELESS MURDER

28. *Dennis Nilsen — strangled his victims as they slept.*

'End of the day. End of drinking. End of a person.'

The unremarkable civil servant was watching the pot on the stove. Dennis had learned catering in Germany with the Royal Fusiliers and specialised in butchering and cooking pork. He was rather partial to the odd wee dram and thought to be addicted to alcohol by the time he left the army in 1972 after ten years' undistinguished service.

Living alone Dennis had a lot of time for reflection as the water in the pot began to boil. His one year's flirtation with the police force had taught him a great deal mund more than once he must have smiled inwardly as he remembered some of the answers he gave at his interview;

"I feel it is my duty to use what talents I have for the benefit of the public at large."

Life as a policeman did not suit Dennis so he moved to the Manpower Services Commission in Denmark Street — near the 'Murder One' Crime Bookshop. Both here and later in Kentish Town he would interview many of the floating population who work in the hotel and catering industry, often mixing business with pleasure inviting the job applicants to a pub or back to his house for a drink.

It was one of these casual workers whose head was boiling in the pot. Nilsen was probably contemplating how to dispose of this particular body, bury it under the floorboards, flush it down the toilet, bury it in the garden or burn it during one of his midnight bonfires.

The modus operandi varied little. Most of his fifteen or so victims were either homosexual or homeless drifters looking for work or accommodation. Nilsen would lure them back to his house with the promise of a bottle of Scotch and strangle them as they tried to sleep off its effects.

It was the disposal of the bodies, possibly the one cooking in the pot which led to his arrest. The grisly residue blocked the drains and neighbours complained of an awful stench. The police were notified after plumbers were brought in and found various human remains.

Nilsen was very forthright and calm in his confessions and informed the police that besides the murders there had been about seven who got away. One of those was traced and he recounted how he sank into a drunken sleep and awoke to find his legs tied together. He also felt something tight around his neck, very tight. Nilsen had his knee on the intended victim's chest and was throttling him with his own tie. The half-strangled Scotsman put up a spirited fight, escaped and phoned the police from a call box. The Metropolitan Police state that they went to interview Nilsen but could not re-contact Douglas Stewart, the complainant, to see if he wished them to proceed with the action.

Two of the other 'escapees' included a Japanese who actually named Nilsen as a would-be killer and a Chinese who escaped after hitting him over the head with a brass candlestick.

Nilsen pleaded not guilty to the six murder and two attempted murder charges, his defence being that he was guilty of manslaughter due to diminished responsibility. Nilsen wrote of his killings;

"The victim is the dirty platter after the feast and the washing up is a clinical ordinary task. It would be better if my reason for killing could be clinically defined — i.e. robbery, jealousy, hate, revenge, sex, blood, lust or sadism.

But it's none of these."

29. *Disposed of the bodies in his back garden.*

He added:

"It amazes me that I have no tears for these victims. I have no tears for myself or those bereaved by my actions."

The only remorse Nilsen showed was for his dog who pined for him after his arrest and died a few days later.

"Poor Mutt" were the killer's only words.

Britain's most prolific mass-murderer was sentenced to six terms of life imprisonment and was not to be released for twenty-five years, well into the twenty-first century.

MARTIN LUPO — THE WOLF MAN

The thirty-seven year old railway guard must have been depressed after his visit to the doctor in the early months of 1986. He had heard the words which terrify all sexually active people today; he was informed that he had AIDS. Little did he know that his life was to be terminated only a few months later in the most brutal manner. The body of James Burns was discovered in a basement in Warwick Road. He had been strangled with a silk stocking or scarf and sexually abused. His tongue had also been bitten off.

The body of Anthony Connolly, another homosexual, was found three weeks later. He had been strangled and the body badly mutilated. Both men used to wear leather jackets and faded jeans, slashed down the leg — a sign that the wearer enjoyed violent sex.

There was a further attack one month later but this time the selected victim fought off his attacker. A homosexual looking for a partner went to Covent Garden with a handsome young man. When they were alone the pick-up produced a black nylon sock and tried to strangle his new acquaintance. The surprised victim struggled and managed to get free as the sock was too short and his attacker ran off. Many people would have been afraid to go to the police as probably happened in the Nilsen case, these being in part responsible for the high number of murders the civil servant committed.

Luckily for other members of the gay community the shaken man went to report the attack and offered to help police in their search by frequenting the gay bars and haunts. The attacker was tracked down and his socks inspected; they were made of silk and bought in Harrods at £20 per pair.

Martin Lupo was certainly not short of money. The ex-choirboy of Italian descent owned a £300,000 house in Kensington and was manager of a Knightsbridge boutique. By night he changed character into the 'wolf-man' having installed his own private torture chamber with iron shackles fitted. He would charge £100 per session for sex and neighbours complained of groans and the clanking of chains emanating from his home. Martin Lupo was an intelligent man speaking five languages but he too was suffering from Aids and the only theory put forward for his attacks was that he was seeking revenge.

The police were shocked when he asked them if they would like to hear about the other murders. One was a vagrant he strangled to death and the other a twenty-two-year-old hospital worker once again strangled, with the tongue bitten off and the body slashed with a rusty razor-blade. He was covered with excrement. Many of the Sunday papers would have liked to have gotten hold of the diaries Lupo kept as they were reported to contain the names of the rich and famous, some in an uncracked code.

Martin Lupo was sentenced to life imprisonment but the judge did not specify how long this should be because he knew of the murderer's illness. The last words on the case should belong to Lupo himself.

"I could say that I'm sorry, but I'm not. I had a clear mind. I knew what I was doing. I was not drunk and I'm not mad."

THE STOCKWELL STRANGLER

Kenneth Erskine had plenty of time to reflect upon his sexual murders. His only visitors whilst he was on remand were solicitors and doctors. Despite lengthy police investigations and the request to the public for help, details as to the twenty-four-year-old's place of abode and lifestyle are still unknown. What is known is that Erskine, who has the mental age of a ten year old, was responsible for the throttling of at least seven pensioners in a four month period between April and July 1986.

Erskine, who was abandoned by his Antiguan born father and English mother, drifted from special school to petty theft and drugtaking. Any proceeds from his burglaries were paid into a building society account. Friendless and homeless, the petty criminal turned to murder, always leaving his victims with their bed clothes pulled up to their chin as if they had died in their sleep. The age range of the victims — four men and three women — varied between 67 and 94. Erskine would break into old people's homes or flats and strangle his victims, sometimes restricting their movement by kneeling on their chest. Most of the victims had been sexually assaulted but their attacker would clear up the scene of his perversions, folding nightwear, tidying the room.

One man survived the attacks and described the few minutes of terror when his throat was squeezed by a man with "black staring eyes and a terrible grin." For no apparent reason the attacker fled and was later picked out at an identity parade by the seventy-four year old retired engineer. He was also spotted leaving the scene of another crime and his palm prints identified from yet another crime. Erskine used to steal any money he could find and entries into his building society accounts tallied with sums stolen from the pensioners.

At his trial he was described as 'a killer who liked killing.' The judge did not want Erskine on the streets again for a very long time and imposed the longest sentence ever set by a judge. The forty years — which will make Erskine a pensioner himself if he is eventually released — were justified by Mr Justice Rose.

"I have no doubt that the horrific nature and number of your crimes requires that I should recommend, taking your age into account, a minimum sentence you must serve."

Erskine began his sentence in January 1988, an unloved, lonely, perverted killer who the prosecution stated had longed for fame. He is a man who lives in a world of his own and who, at times, cannot distinguish between reality and fantasy.

MURDER 'ORRIBLE MURDER.

The working classes of Victorian England were fascinated by gruesome tales from around the world. Labourers in the London factories would often pay a boy to read a copy of THE ILLUSTRATED POLICE NEWS as they worked and would stare in disbelief at the somewhat imaginative illustrations. It was rare for the artist to visit the scene of the drama but the fine wood carvings are in many ways excellent illustrations, being lively, melodramatic and to our twentieth century eyes often grimly funny. All the illustrations date from the 1860s or 1870s.

31. The murder of Fanny Adams.

30. One of the more imaginative illustrations.

Some of the headlines are not dissimilar to today's tabloids;

"Shutting a woman's head in a box."
"Killed by a coffin."
"A child stolen by a monkey."
"A woman raised from the dead."
"Fearful encounter with a boa constrictor."
"Horrible cannibalism."
"Horrible discovery of a girl eaten by rats."
"A boy mistaken for a crow."
and "A wife driven insane by husband tickling her feet."

Let's take a look at some of the reports, though as in some of today's tabloids the veracity of the story has not been fully checked.

32. The girls prefer the Thames to life as 'respectable servant'.

A deplorable mystery of London was investigated by a coroner's jury on Monday last, the report of which will be found below.

Early on Friday morning a lock-keeper, not far from the Queen's Road Bridge over the Regent's Canal at Dalston heard screams and splashing in the water. Going at once to the spot with the drags, he, after some delay drew out the dead body of a girl. Meanwhile the police also became aware that there had been a suicide at the bridge and set to work in search of the bodies and by and by they brought out two young women, stark and dead, the hand of one clutching with a convulsive grip the hair of the other. Of the three unhappy creatures, none of them more than seventeen or eighteen, little is known except that, as they lie rigid and still on the deadhouse table, their sodden garments seem to indicate that they were once "respectable servants." Once! for those humble, laborious days were over, and the night before the suicide was spent — as the respectable and virtuous do not spend their nights. At a late hour the three unfortunate girls had been seen sitting in the street, drinking from a bottle; trying it may be, to drown the cruel memory of the past, or forget the misery of the present, or nerve themselves for their leap into the future — for already the threats of self murder were on their lips. Then they were seen upon the bridge, sitting on the parapet. One threw some papers to another young girl not far off with the request that they be taken to her father and that they should tell him "Esther was with me". They then joined hands and clasped each other's wrists; and the water and the night hid the last wrestle these three girls — not yet much more than children — had with a life that was too hard for them. They must no doubt have been wicked; most reprehensible and shocking in the eyes of all proper persons. Yet perhaps, the rush into the unknown was prompted by something like repentant horror at what they knew — perhaps being bad enough already, they chose to die rather than grow worse, and that is a choice which even the righteous would not always find it easy to make.

DEATH FROM SWALLOWING A MOUSE

33. All stories were verified!

A most extraordinary occurrence was brought to light a few days ago at an inquest held on the body of a man in South London. From the evidence it appears that in a workroom where the many young girls were at work, a mouse suddenly made its appearance on a table causing of course, considerable commotion. The intruder was seized, however, by a young man who happened to be present, but the mouse slipped out of his hand and running up his sleeve, came out between his waistcoat and shirt at the neck. The unfortunate man had his mouth open and the mouse darted thither, and in his fright and surprise the man actually swallowed it. That a mouse can exist for a considerable time without much air has long been a popular belief, and was unfortunately proved to be a fact in the present instance, for the mouse began to tear and gnaw inside the man's throat and chest and the unfortunate fellow died after a little while in the most horrible agony. Several witnesses having corroborated the above facts and medical evidence having been given as to the cause of death, a verdict of accidental death was returned. The mouse has been preserved in spirits of wine and has been placed in the Museum of London Hospital.

We cannot leave the Illustrated Police News without the report of a murder. Though the following case did not take place in the capital it does help show the primitive beliefs still held amongst country folk little more than a hundred years ago.

KILLING A SUPPOSED WITCH

A very singular charge of murder was tried at Warwick Assizes last week, before Baron Bramwell. James Haywood, agricultural labourer, forty years of age and a Wesleyan, was charged with the wilful murder of Anne Tennent, at Long Compton, Warwickshire. It was proved in evidence that fully one third of the villagers believed in witchcraft. The prisoner believing in the common superstition, stabbed the deceased, who was eighty years of age, with a pitchfork, under the impression she was one of the fifteen witches he ought to kill. It was admitted that on all other subjects he was sane. He justified his conduct by referring to verses from Leviticus: "A man also or woman that hath a familiar spirit, or that is a wizard, should be put to death; they shall stone them with stones; their blood shall be upon them." The Judge said that such a prevalence of this superstition would be disgraceful to savages. The prisoner was found to have been insane at the time, and was ordered to be kept in confinement during Her Majesty's pleasure.

KILLING A SUPPOSED WITCH

34. One of the many murder cases.

READING

If Londoners found some of the stories in the 'Illustrated Police News' a little too gory they might have been found engrossed in one of the following books all published in the capital in the nineteenth century. We have no accurate figures to show how well they sold;

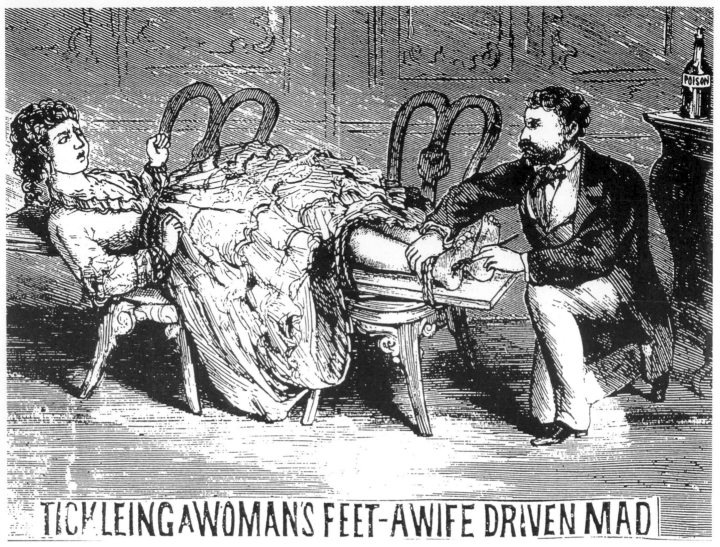

TICKLEING A WOMANS FEET - A WIFE DRIVEN MAD

35. *Tied to a plank and cruelly ill-treated by her uncle Mrs. Puckeridge was taken to the workhouse where she was placed with other insane patients.*

"SWEET SLEEP. A COURSE OF READING INTENDED TO PROMOTE THAT DELIGHTFUL ENJOYMENT." The book includes a chapter on 'The Polite Arts of Yawning and Snoring."

"NEW TEETH FOR OLD JAWS: BOOKSELLING SPIRITUALISED."

"THE LITTLE I SAW OF CUBA."

"HOW TO BOIL WATER IN A PAPER BAG."

"WED TO A LUNATIC. A WILD, WEIRD YARN OF LOVE AND SOME OTHER THINGS DELIVERED IN THE FORM OF HASH FOR THE BENEFIT OF TIRED READERS."

"CRAB, SHRIMP AND LOBSTER LORE."

"BEARD SHAVING, AND THE COMMON USE OF THE RAZOR, AN UNNATURAL, IRRATIONAL, UNMANLY, UNGODLY AND FATAL FASHION AMONG CHRISTIANS."

"OCTOGENERIAL TEETOTALLERS, WITH ONE HUNDRED AND THIRTEEN PORTRAITS" and "CRIMINAL LIFE: REMINISCENCES OF FORTY-TWO YEARS AS A POLICE OFFICER" by Superintendent James Bent.

A CAUTIONARY TALE

When researching into the darker side of London's history in old documents, magazines and newspapers it is very easy to get side-tracked into reading the other news of the day which often proves more rewarding and entertaining. The story below, taken from a newspaper in 1888, has probably not been re-told since. The facts certainly seem stranger than fiction and the tale still worth telling over one hundred years later.

Seeking to take advantage of the London Insurance market a German, living in France, insured his life for no less a sum than £14,000. He provided a photograph of himself but very little else, as, right from the start, his intention was to swindle the insurers.

For this purpose he needed a false death certificate and therefore accomplices, the main one being a 'widow' to receive the money after his payment of just one premium. He had no trouble finding a willing accomplice to do the job but then had the thornier problem of finding a 'body' which resembled his own, to prove he had in fact died.

The German began a tour of the hospices of Paris and finally found a consumptive patient who bore some resemblance to himself. The question was posed;

> "Is there no chance for him, poor fellow, if he was taken away to the seaside and tenderly nurtured?"

> "There might just be the shadow of a chance, but he has no friends" the doctor replied.

> "Then I shall be his friend."

With the great admiration of the hospital staff the German philanthropist whisks the patient off to his residence by the sea.

So far events were going to plan but the first of many quirks was to befall the potential swindler. Against all expectations the sea air does revive the patient and he shows distinct signs of recovery!

The patient did however die and there was strong suspicion that his death may have been assisted by the German though this was never proved. When alive the sick man had resembled the benefactor who at his own expense had taken him to the seaside but after death the resemblance disappeared.

"Why now he is not one bit like your photograph" exclaimed the 'widow'.

"We'll soon remedy that" the quick-witted German replied; upon which he dressed himself in grave clothes, whitened his face and had his photograph taken.

Why he did not do this in the first place will remain an unanswered mystery. All that was now needed was a certificate of death. For a fee in the region of £1,000 he was able to bribe a French doctor friend to furnish him the necessary papers. These were duly dispatched to London and the £14,000 returned to the 'widow!'

All three collaborators, flushed with their success used to talk unreservedly of their excellent stroke of business. As they spoke in German they thought it was safe to discuss the case in front of their maid. Little did they know she could understand their language but had no intention of revealing what she knew until the Doctor made certain unwanted 'proposals' to the girl which she found offensive.

Unfortunately for the perpetrators of the fraud the maid was engaged to a Parisian journalist. She wrote to him revealing everything and he immediately set off to London to tip off the insurance companies.

The German philanthropist, his widow and their doctor, fled France. The pursuit was intermittent but persistent and they were eventually run to earth. The German had no hesitation in committing suicide and the other two malefactors given terms of imprisonment.

What makes the case stranger than fiction is that the day after the German's suicide a letter arrived for him saying he had inherited a large fortune.

Was it the fault of these fraudsters of old that we have to fill in so many forms and wait so long for the finicky insurance companies to meet their claims today?

36. *Execution outside Newgate. The prisoner shouted: 'I am innocent. Cut my head off but don't hang me'.*

LEISURE

Leisure activities were a great release from the humdrum of everyday life in the Middle Ages. Early forms of football and handball were enjoyed though rules tended to be made up as the game was played. During the Hundred Years War the capital's inhabitants were encouraged to practise their fighting skills. Londoners would do battle with all types of weapon until blood was drawn. The practice of archery was positively encouraged by an Act in 1369

"that everyone of the said City of London strong in body at leisure times and on holidays, use in their recreation bows and arrows."

Some of the arrows were capable of penetrating a 4″ oak door. If an archer killed a person by accident while practising he was not punished.

Wrestling was popular in London with a prize of bags of money being thrown into the ring by the Lord Mayor. This was often followed to the amusement of all those present by a parcel of wild rabbits being released. Mayhem would break out amongst the audience as they endeavoured to capture a free supper.

The Stuarts seemed to derive a perverse pleasure in being cruel to animals. Cats were hung in baskets to be used as targets and they were often stuffed alive and placed on bonfires. Inflated bladders were sometimes tied to the poor cat's back and the animal thrown out of the window to see how far it could 'fly'.

37. *Cruelty to animals was 'entertainment' for some.*

Badgers were tied into holes in the ground and set upon by dogs. Their strong jaws often killed 5 or 6 before they died, often from exhaustion.

One Frenchman in the capital over two hundred years ago observed that:

"anything that looks like a fight was delicious to an Englishman."

There was a great deal of betting on bare-knuckle boxing and if the fight was going against one gambler he would often join in, kicking and punching to try and save his wager. It was for this reason we have the raised stage today.

Fighting was not just confined to the male sex as we can witness from this graphic description by Cesar de Saussure;

"Both women were scantily clothed, and wore little bodices and very short petticoats of white linen. One of those amazons was a stout Irishwoman, strong and lithe to look at, the other was a small Englishwoman, full of fire and very agile. The first was decked with blue ribbons on the head, waist and right arm; the second wore red ribbons. Their weapons were a sort of two-handed sword, three or four and a half feet in length; the guard was covered, and the blade was about three inches wide and not sharp, only about half a foot of it was, but then that part cut like a razor. The spectators made numerous bets and some peers who were there laid some very large wagers. On either side of the two amazons a man stood by, holding a long staff, ready to separate them should blood flow. After a time the combat became very animated, and was conducted with force and vigour with the broad side of the weapons. The Irishwoman presently received a great cut across her forehead, and that put a stop to the first part of the combat. The Englishwoman's backers threw her shillings and half-crowns and applauded her. During this time the wounded woman's forehead was sewn up, this being done on stage; a plaster was applied to it, and she drank a big glass of spirits to revive her courage, and the fight began again, each combatant holding a dagger in her left hand to ward off the blows. The Irishwoman was wounded a second time and her adversary again received coins and plaudits from her admirers. The wound was sewn up, and for the third time the battle recommenced . . . The poor Irishwoman was destined to be the loser, for she received a long and deep wound across her neck and throat. The surgeon sewed it up, but she was too badly hurt to fight any more, and it was time, for the combatants were dripping with perspiration, and the Irishwoman also with blood. A few coins were thrown to her to console her, but the victor made a good day's work out of the combat."

Not all fights were organised. There is a contemporary description of a fight in Drury Lane between "two she-devils engaged in a scratching and boxing match, their faces entirely covered with blood, their bosoms bare and the clothes torn from their bodies."

Gambling was as popular throughout London's history as it is today. As far as fighting was concerned there was even a kind of handicap system where one man was pitched against two or three women. It was not uncommon for animals to be involved in the handicap system.

38. *Beer and clay pipes, 1877.*

Betting was not just confined to fighting and racing. Walpole tells the story of a man being observed falling down in the street. Bets were placed as to whether he was dead or not. When a passer-by suggested they should assist him by bleeding the man, the gamblers protested that this would prejudice their bet. Long term wagers were made in the men's clubs and if one went through the "books" it would not be uncommon to discover gambles on how long certain wars would last or the ages at which certain prominent people would die. There was even a bet of £3,000 struck as to which of two raindrops would first reach the bottom of the windowpane.

Even Royalty were fond of a gamble and during a carriage journey down Bond Street Charles James Fox struck a bet with the Prince of Wales as to how many cats would be seen on each side of the street. Fox chose the sunny side and won the bet thirteen to none.

There was no greater treat for Londoners on their few public holidays than to let themselves go at one of the many annual fairs. One of the biggest attractions was always the freak show, be they either human or animal, this continuing late into the nineteenth century with the exhibition of The Elephant Man, whose skeleton is in the London Hospital. The Society for the Suppression of Vice and the R.S.P.C.A. were founded at the start of the 19th century to try to protect some of the 'exhibits' but did not at first receive a great deal of support from the general public. The number of human freaks (dwarfs, giants etc) at Bartholomew Fair did decrease from eighteen to fifteen after the founding of these societies and the animals (exhibits of freaks and menageries etc) from thirty-seven to twenty-five. What exactly were these exhibits?

For a price in the 1700s you could have seen 'The Mare with Seven Feet' and 'Toby' the pig that knew the alphabet, could tell the time and do accounts. There was a family of learned cats and probably the most educated of all — The Scientific 'Java Sparrows,' all Oxford undergraduates and capable of speaking seven languages. The unacceptable face of animal exploitation was also very much in evidence in side streets with cock-fighting, dog-fighting, badger-baiting and ratting appealing to all walks of London life.

The human freaks included 'the amazing little Dwarf, 'the American Dwarf' the 'Tall Lady from Norfolk and The Short One from Durham'. The London mobs' stereotyped views of foreigners were reinforced with negro 'cannibals' and 'inhuman Turks'. Chinese sewing-needle swallowers were of perennial interest. One visitor to Croydon describes his meeting with the bearded lady:

"This woman presented for our admiration a large full beard, a foot long and more, growing upon the whole of her face, cheeks chin and lip, so that her mouth was quite hidden by it. She was by this time unfortunately, fully fifty years of age, and her beard well grizzled, so that we had no opportunity of knowing how a woman in her youth and beauty would look with such an ornament to her face . . . This woman was a great strong creature who might have felled an ox with her fist; she had a deep voice and a merry laugh, and made no opposition when Jack offered her a glass.''

The fascinated visitor goes on to describe some of the other attractions;

'We saw the Irish giant, also, who was a mighty tall fellow but weak in the knees; and the strong woman who tossed about the heavy weights as if they had been made of pasteboard, and lifted great stones with her hair, and, since where there are giants there must also be dwarfs, we saw the Italian Fairy, a girl of sixteen no taller than eighteen inches, and said to be a princess in her own country . . . This little creature, dressed in a flowered petticoat and a frock of sarsnet, walked about her stage, carried herself and spoke with all the airs of a court lady though where she learnt these arts I know not.'

With a largely illiterate audience most entertainment had to be visual. There was an insatiable demand for gory and macabre exhibitions, these ranging from waxwork figures of recent murderers to complete re-enactments of their crimes, with puppets carrying out mock executions. The murder of Maria Marten in the Red Barn was one of the most popular 'panoramics'. The play is still being performed today. Peep shows were big money-earners and after The William Rush murders in 1849 all 'box office' records were broken.

The atmosphere of the fairs can best be demonstrated with contemporary reports, so let's rejoin our friend at Croydon Fair: 'And before every show were ballad singers bawling their songs. Their principal business at fairs is not, I am told, to sell their ballads so much as to attract a crowd and engage their attention while the scoundrel pickpockets go about their business unwatched (one was caught in the fair while we were there, and for want of a pump, was put head first into a tub of water, and kept there till he was well-nigh drowned): and everywhere there were men who grinned and postured, girls who danced, boys who walked on stilts, gipsies who told fortunes, women balling brandy-balls and hot furmety; there was the hobby-horse man with his trumpet and his "Troop, every one, one, one!" and a hundred more too numerous to mention. For food they had booths where they sold hot roast pork, with bread and onions and black porter, a banquet to which the gentry at the fair, whose stomachs are not queasy, did infinite justice.'

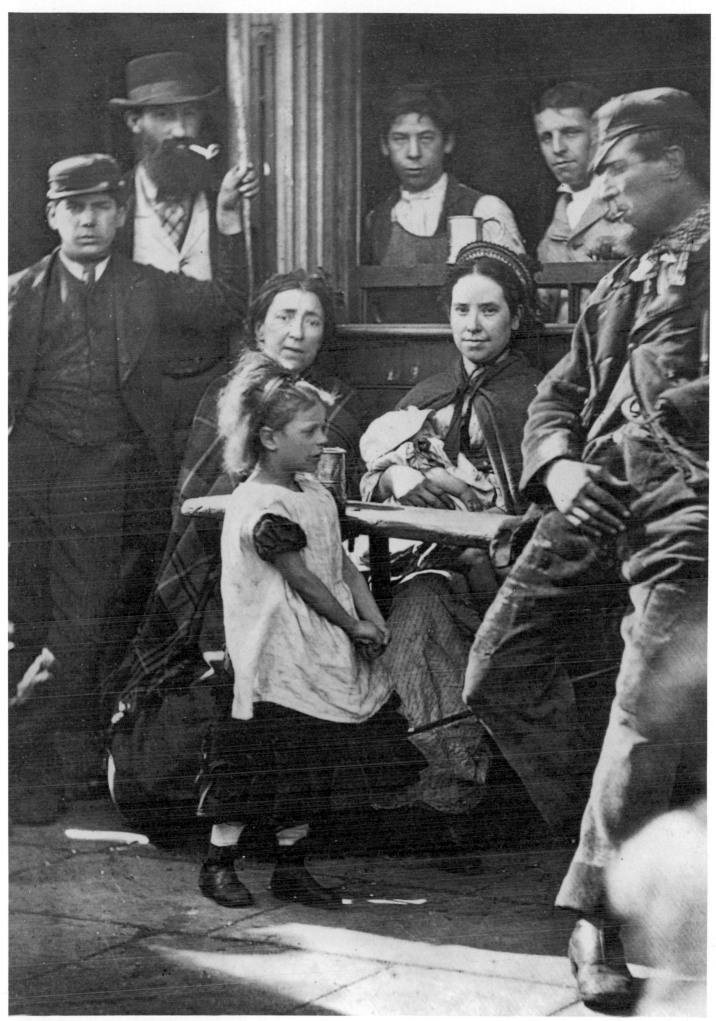

39. *Hookey Alf of Whitechapel, 1877. There were no age restrictions for going to the pub.*

40. *Reading — one of the most popular Victorian pastimes.*

One of the ballads the writer mentions creates a very vivid picture of the activities at Bow Fair in 1800.

There's dancing, kissing, courting too,
and a great many more such things to do,
getting drunk I do declare,
when they go to see Bow Fair.

There's hallowing, singing, cracking nuts,
some cramming sausages down their guts,
Gin and gingerbread, I do declare,
is what they get when they go to Bow Fair.

Another verse from 'The Humours of Bow Fair' describes the colourful characters:

. . . The watermen with Wapping whores
over the fields do come by scores
From Billingsgate comes fish fag Nan
some Thames Street Carman is her flash man
Soft-cinder Sue, scavenger Dick,
Both arm in arm doth fondly trip . . .

The fairs in some senses gave way to the music halls which were forever being attacked from the pulpits around the capital. Dickens described Sadlers Wells as 'a beer garden resounding with foul language, oaths, cat-calls, shrieks, yells, blasphemy, obscenity.'

You could also go to a "cock and hen" club where men and women met to sing songs or to one of the 'Penny gaffs': these were rooms on the upper floor of shops where obscene dances were performed and coarse songs sung. It was said that 'the most immoral acts' were represented. Saucy drawings of the 'actors' and actresses were displayed to entice prospective customers.

MR JAMRACH'S

There was no way that even the most unobservant Eastender could have walked down St George's Street East in Bow without noticing something a little out of the ordinary; be it the roar of a lion, the screeching of thousands of birds or the sight of a boa-constrictor wrapped around the portly body of the proprietor, Mr Charles Jamrach. His museum/shop/menagerie was one of the most fascinating places in the capital with the owner's name Jamrach being accepted into East End language to signify 'a social assemblage of mixed characters and uncertain pedigrees.'

Mr Jamrach was a great naturalist and very learned as far as animal behaviour was concerned. Thrice married he wondered why one of his wives objected to his keeping boa-constrictors under the bed. He was an importer, breeder and exporter of all kinds of animals who supplied travelling menageries and scientific collections. Mr Jamrach showed particular interest in the breeding of long-coated Persian greyhounds, Japanese pugs and Madagascar cats. He also kept young lions, tigers and dwarf cattle from Burmah. The exotic collection was not limited solely to animals for Mr Jamrach was a great collector and dealer of objects with customers from all walks of life.

Just wandering around the poorly-lit buildings you might come across strange barbaric weapons, spears from the South Seas, poison-tipped arrows, eerie shields, strangely carved tusks of elephants, dusty old cabinets bearing grinning gods and nodding idols and strange beings in glass cases such as demons coiled up in bottles.

The warehouse held even more treasures; Japanese cabinets bristling with charms for headaches and toothaches, heartburns and cut fingers, chunks of lapis-lazuli and greenstones from New Zealand. There are vases from all over the world, a hideous Fijian war-mask lies next to the Buddha. Many of the glass-cases are thick with dust. Mr Jamrach is in no hurry to sell as he knows many articles appreciate with age.

The main attractions of the premises however are the live exhibitions and it would be fitting for their owner to tell you about them himself. These extracts are taken from the PALL MALL BUDGET from 1890.

"Snakes are not so valuable as they were, you may have him (a python) for three pounds. Time was when he was worth fifteen.

The best elephants come from Burmah. Two or three years ago I bought twenty of them. But now I would not take one as a gift, for they eat their heads off, and are very delicate.

We seldom have an accident. They (Lions and Tigers) come over in a cage, are slung over the ship's side on to the waggon, brought up here, and the cage is placed face to face with another cage of which the door is open. A tempting piece of meat lies on the floor, and the beast which is generally hungry, rushes to the bait and is trapped without trouble. I remember many years ago a rather startling adventure. A tiger got loose close by here, and walked off down the street. A little boy who was watching the operation went up to the tiger, who was looking about him with some curiosity, and patted him on the back. The tiger took the little boy up in his mouth and carried him off down the street. I made for the beast and throwing my arms around his neck pinned him to the ground, the boy was rescued, the tiger stunned by a crack to the head.

Last year I had three or four thousand birds flying about loose in here, but now I just have a few in stock, and these are divided. Here are piping crows, blear-eyed cockatoos, Amazon parrots, rosy-faced love-birds, and there is the bul-bul that Tom Moore raved about, the Siberian waxwing, the black-throated grakle, pagoda starling, New Zealand paroquets and many many more!"

After Mr Jamrach's death the business was passed on to his son and when he died in 1917 the stock was sold off over a period of five years.

A copy of one of the many invoices may make entertaining reading:-

Two hump-backed camels	£30
Spotted hyenas	£30 a pair
One peccary	£4
Two mongooses	£1 each
Spider monkey	£3
Two baboons	£20 a pair
Mesopotania deer	£10 each
Porcupine	£5
Bengal tiger cat	£4
South American ocelot	£2
Pair of Persian greyhounds	£40
Full-grown cassowary	£40
Great Eagle Owl	£4
Four pelicans	£5 each

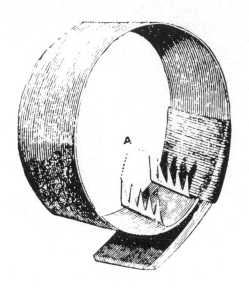

41. Anti-masturbation devices, 1877.

In medieval times the 'red-light' area was in Southwark, by the river, so the area was out of the jurisdiction of the City of London. Before the days of rather more subtle advertising the prospective customer was left in little doubt as to local industry when he found himself in streets with names such as Gropecunt Lane. The local inns called 'The Bell' or 'The Castle' doubled up as brothels.

The church did its utmost to try and take the pleasure away from the most natural of pastimes but as today most people went their own way. In the seventeenth century it was feared that masturbation was getting out of hand, the practice being so common it became known as the "English Disease". Both girls and boys were taught that it led to, amongst other things, boils, epilepsy, convulsions, indigestion and even death. As we know in these enlightened days this is a lot of nonsense, its only noticeable effect being deafness! In the nineteenth century all manner of machines and contraptions were devised to prevent boys from playing with themselves. These included a device with spikes attached to the penis at night to prevent them from taking matters into their own hands. There was another contraption which was attached to the same area and was connected to the parents' bedroom to alert them if their son had an erection.

In Baden-Powell's Scouts handbook 'Rovering To Success' he gives warnings about masturbation; 'It cheats semen of getting its full chance of making up the strongly manly man you would otherwise be. You are throwing away the seed that has been handed down to you as a trust instead of keeping it and ripening it for bringing a son to you later on.'

So all of you who are not manly men, you now know the reason!

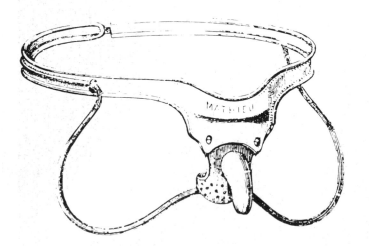
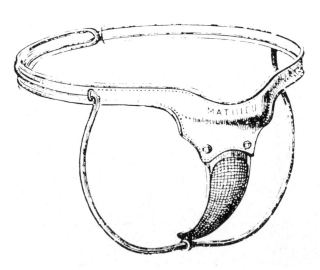

42. By 1904 equality for the sexes. Male and female anti-masturbation devices.

43. *A daring photograph for the early twentieth century.*

44. *Discreet shoe-fitting device.*

There were often degrading sexual initiation ceremonies in London factories when thirteen-year-olds started work. One man remembers having his trousers pulled down and his penis greased and massaged by the other young workers. Horse manure was then added and comprehensively rubbed in.

Weddings in London in the seventeenth century were often conducted in the Fleet area. There were signs outside buildings with illustrations of a man and a woman holding hands to show that marriages were performed within. Touts would go scouring the capital looking for trade and receive a commission on any wedding fee received. The marriages were often carried out by clergymen imprisoned in the Fleet, an extremely expensive establishment at the time.

The age of consent was fourteen for boys and twelve years old for girls and it was customary for the bride to wear gloves in bed. Many of the men wore tight breeches which were said to be appreciated by the women as 'It lets us know what they are thinking about.'

All sorts of clubs sprang up in London over the centuries, and there were publications to help the foreign visitor including 'The Whoremonger's Guide to London' and a 'List of Covent Garden Ladies!'

The homosexual population was also catered for in a club where:

"The men (were) calling one another 'my dear' and hugging, kissing and tickling each other, as they were a mixture of wanton males and females, some telling each other they ought to be whipped for not coming to school more frequently."

There were also flagellants' clubs in Jermyn Street for those who had still not quite gotten over their schoolday beatings. At the top end of the market, with sufficient funds, one could seek entertainment in any one of the many expensive high class brothels. They would put on special shows with 'twelve virgins' and twelve 'able youths' and the audience encouraged to participate before the end of the two hour shows.

One of the most famous brothels, frequented by Sheridan, was run by Miss Fawklands. Composed of three houses, the first building was known as 'The Temple of Aurora'. Here twelve young girls aged between eleven and sixteen entertained old men, though no sexual intercourse was allowed. In the second house older, more experienced women catered for the needs of those wanting a little more entertainment. In the third every whim was satisfied by the most skilled women on the premises a man could have.

One of Victoria's Prime Ministers who she strongly disliked would go out into the East End and invite young female down-and-outs back to his residence. It is unknown whether Gladstone did anything more than lecture them but he was very highly sexed and hated himself for these feelings.

The age of consent was raised from 12 to 13 in 1871 and to 16 in 1885. Very little sex-education was imparted until the nineteen sixties. Many girls did not know what was happening at the onset of menstruation. Some thought they were dying, others felt ashamed and made do with pieces of rag or sheets. In some of the religious schools girls had to bath under a towel or in their underwear as it was thought to be a sin to look at one's own body.

THE TRIAL AND
EXECUTION

OF

CAPT. HENRY NICHOLS,

Who Suffered this Morning,

AT

MY thoughts on awful subjects roll,
Damnation and the dead ;
What horrors seize the guilty soul
Upon a dying bed!
Lingering about these mortal shores,
She makes a long delay,
Till, like a flood, with rapid force
Death sweeps the wretch away.

Then swift and dreadful he decends
Down to the fiery coast,
Amongst abominable fiends,
Himself a frightful ghost.

There endless crowds of sinners lie,
And darkness makes their chains ;
Tortur'd with keen despair they cry,
Yet wait for fiercer pains.

HORSEMONGER LANE GOAL, SOUTHWARK.

HEINOUS, horribly frightful, and disgusting was the crime for which the above poor Wretched Culprit suffered the severe penalty of the law this morning, Monday, August 12, 1833, at the top of Horsemonger Lane Goal. His name became known to the public during the investigation relative to the death of the unfortunate boy Paviour, who was lately, it is suspected, so inhumanely murdered by a Gang of Miscreants. He was also spoken of, as being concerned with a Captain Beauclerk, who destroyed himself while in Horsemonger Lane Goal, some months ago.

Thank Heavens, the public Gallows of Justice in England is very rarely disgraced by the Execution of such Wretches ; but, every person must have observed, with dismay, how greatly the number of diabolical assaults of a similar nature, have lately multiplied in this country.

His TRIAL took place at Croydon, on Friday, August 2, before the Honourable Sir James Parke, when the Jury returned a Verdict of GUILTY, on the clearest possible evidence : the statement of the boy Lawrence, with whom the offence was committed, was very clear. It was confirmed by the testimony of a person connected with Capt. Beauclerk.

The Judge immediately pronounced the dreadful sentence of the Law, advising him to make all the atonement in his power to an offended GOD, the few days he had to live ; for, he might rest assured, the sentence would not be mitigated.

Captain Nichols displayed the greatest calmness, and was unmoved throughout the Trial, and even when the dreadful sentence was passed, he remained perfectly collected.

At nine o'clock this morning the full penalty of the law was carried into effect upon the above individual. Upon being brought back from Croydon to Horsemonger-lane he devoted nearly the whole of the time left him in making his peace with his Creator. On the sheriff going to demand his body he was in the chapel with the Rev. Mr. Mann, the chaplain of the goal, and in a firm voice he informed that gentleman that he was satisfied with his sentence, and was fully prepared to die. He trusted that he had found mercy in his God, and that his crime would be forgiven. So firm was his faith, that he did wish to live another hour. In the course of these observations, the rev. gentleman happened to sigh, on which the culprit said, " Do not sigh." Upon seeing Mr. Walters, the governor, he took that gentleman by the hand, and said, " Although an unfavourable impression existed against him in the prison, he had to thank him and the goalers for their tenderness and humanity towards him." He then turned round, and said, " I am ready." On walking along, the bell was being tolled, when he begged that it might be stopped. He then walked with a remarkably firm step to the drop, and in a few minutes he ceased to exist. He apparently died instantaneously. The culprit, who is fifty years of age, was a remarkably fine looking man, and we understand had served in the Peninsular war, and was of a very respectable family. Since his apprehension not a single member of his family ever visited him, and we understand that it is not their intention to demand the corpse. Under these circumstances the body will be sent to one of the hospitals.

Emerton Printer, Looley Street.

45. Hanged for homosexuality.

It appears that if men were presentable and left a little gift they could tour the capital touching any young woman who took their fancy. In 1762 James Boswell toured London in search of sex, the only qualification being that his partner was female be they 'jolly young damsels' or 'strong, plump, good-humoured girls'. There was a predilection for sex 'al fresco' with Boswell describing one of his conquests on Westminster Bridge. Pepys and Johnson described many similar matings.

Women were still very much second-class citizens and quite often sold on the open market. A report on Smithfield Market in the Times states:

> 'By an oversight in the report we are not in a position to quote this week the price of women. The increasing value of the fairer sex is considered by various celebrated writers to be a sure sign of increasing civilization.'

Pornography is as old as the capital itself, most of the literature coming from France. Pepys admits to having enjoyed it in the seventeenth century and in his own cryptic style with a mixture of English and Latin-based languages he noted;

> 'It did hazard my prick para stand all the while . . . and una vez to decharger.'

Two hundred years later the British Prime Minister was reading similar material but atoned by whipping himself afterwards.

Dildoes imported from Italy were for sale in St James's St in the 18th century and condoms or 'English overcoats' utilised by many of the richer classes, not to avoid conception but the ubiquitous gonorrhoea. These sheaths were made from fish skin or sheep gut and secured by a red ribbon tied around the scrotum. Although not sounding too appealing, the alternative — risking 'the pox' was a real deterrent. The cure in those times was by applying camphor liniment and mercury plaster to the genitals. There were no end of 'quack' cures with one common trait — they were all expensive.

To avoid conception men resorted to bathing their penises in vinegar or henbane juice and women were advised to use douches of oil, camphor and rue. Conception was also thought to be less likely if intercourse was performed 'with much violent activity'!

Virgins were very much in demand being thought to cure venereal disease and Irish maidens looking for work were often procured and 'sold' for extremely high prices.

The sexual behaviour of some of the capital's most famous inhabitants make for rather entertaining reading. George the Second had his coffin constructed so that when it was laid next to his wife Caroline's the sides could be removed and the bones would be coupled for ever.

For most of the last ten years of his reign George III was an embarrassment to the country being almost totally insane. He would often expose himself and shout for the Queen to satisfy him. He would on other occasions smack the bottom of a pretty, respectable lady and exclaim 'what a pretty arse'.

He met his match one day whilst ogling the breasts of one of the attractive young ladies at court. She asked him if he would like her to put his hands on something soft. It was an offer the salivating king could not refuse and the young lady took hold of his hands and placed them on his head!

Queen Victoria enjoyed a healthy sex-life until the death of her beloved Albert which she never quite got over. She had an exact replica of his hand made of plaster and took it to bed with her every night along with his pyjamas which she would clutch to her bosom. It was only in the last ten years of her life that the maid was able to remove them after the Queen fell asleep. It was this same monarch who said to her eldest daughter that women were born for man's pleasure and amusement.

Victorian pornography, aimed at the middle-class male was mostly verbal in content and featured stories about the 'de-flowering' of lower-class women, especially servants and country girls and even children. Indeed it was not uncommon for a maid's first sexual encounters to take place with one of the males in the household where she worked.

In the early years of the twentieth century it was thought correct that children should have no contact with the opposite sex. Separate schools with high fences were built and a severe thrashing was possible for just talking to a member of the opposite sex.

This segregation was probably enforced after the studies of London pupils' home life where Beatrice Webb noted;

> "To put it bluntly, sexual promiscuity and even sexual perversion, are almost unavoidable amongst men and women of average character and intelligence crowded into the one-room tenement of slum areas."

Even in her autobiography written as late as 1926 Ms Webb observes;

> "The fact that some of my workmates — young girls, who were in no way mentally defective; who were, on the contrary, just as keen-witted and generous-hearted as my own circle of friends — could chaff each other about having babies by their fathers and brothers, was a gruesome example of the effect of debased social environment on personal character and family life."

Charles Booth had previously hinted at the problem;

> "Drink is fostered by bad houses . . .
> Crowded houses send men to the public houses . . .
> Crowding is the main cause of drink and vice . . .
> Incest is common resulting from over-crowding . . ."

Because of the lack of sex-education most youngsters were taught the facts of life by somebody a little older but not always wiser. Annie Besant married 'with no more idea of the marriage relation than if I had been four years old instead of twenty.' Even in a survey conducted as recently as 1949 eighty per cent of females of child-bearing age were found to have had no sex-education and there are even stories of pregnant women who thought the baby made its exit via the navel.

FOOD AND DRINK

46. *Mealtimes can be stressful.*

47. Fish and potato salesman — East End.

The Londoner's diet in the past, as today, varied according to status and purchasing power. Little did the Romans know that their eating and drinking habits would contribute to their eventual demise. Many of the leaders suffered from lead poisoning contracted from pewter dishes made with an alloy of lead. The wine, so popular in those days, was prevented from going sour by the addition of syrup — boiled in lead-lined pots. Death was slow but sure with the victim becoming listless before just fading away. The Romans brought hundreds of plants, herbs and flowers, and orchards of cherry trees grew where the armies spat out the stones.

A centurion would consider it a treat to be served with dormice baked in honey and crushed spices. One of the showpieces of the time was a large pastry pie which when cut open would release small live birds which then took wing. They were followed by the Romans themselves in about 400 AD.

The British carried on experimenting and many more birds were eaten than is the case today. It was not uncommon to be served peacock, blackbird, rook or crow and at a banquet you might have savoured a roast swan dressed with its own feathers, stuffed with a capon, stuffed in turn with a partridge, a lark and a wren.

The poorer peasant's lot did not change a great deal over the centuries, he having to survive on oat gruel for breakfast, and pottage with a little home-made bread to fend off the hunger pangs at other times. The cauldron was also used for washing clothes and the yearly bath.

The Londoners lucky enough to live near The Thames may have supplemented their diet with 'fat, sweet salmon . . . daily taken from it and no other river in Europa had such store of barbels, trouts, roaches, dace, gudgeon, flounder and shrimps'.

Londoners in the seventeenth century did not follow a very healthy regime, eating few vegetables and little fruit with most dairy products being consumed in the country. The diet consisted mostly of bread, pastry, meat, poultry, fish and all kinds of sweetmeats. The London women were described as 'sweetly pretty but for their black teeth'. Spots and blemishes were covered by 'beauty patches' which became more and more elaborate, some even taking the design of a coach-and-horses.

Tea drinking in Stuart times was very much a luxury and highly taxed. Londoners were the first to take up the habit and a story which caused much amusement at the time concerns a package of tea sent to a friend in the country by one of the capital's inhabitants.

There were no instructions with the present so the country lady boiled the leaves and served them with salt and butter to the expectant guests at her tea-party, the water being thrown away. Needless to say the gathering was not over-impressed with the new taste and vowed never to touch it again. The British have always been seen as a rather eccentric tea-drinking nation. This view would have been reienforced by any foreigner in Trafalgar Square just before Nelson was to take up his position. There was a tea-party taking place at the top of the column.

Tea-leaves, albeit third hand, began to make their way down through the servants to the poorer classes. The hot water needed to brew destroyed the germs as much as the alcohol in their other favourite tipple, beer, and without knowing why those who drank these had a better chance of good health than those drinking the contaminated water. It wasn't to last for long. The introduction of gin and a vast increase in the capital's population brought serious health problems as we shall witness later. Many drinking clubs were formed with just one rule; that all the members should get drunk. Tea was certainly not flavour of the month amongst the club members who denounced it as 'scandal broth'. There were also those opposed to the introduction of coffee on the grounds that it was an anti-aphrodisiac and known in some circles as 'eunuchs drink'. Egg and spices were often added to the drinking chocolate which was growing in popularity.

In the seventeenth century it became customary to have a draught of ale or wine around 11am, both being warmed in winter; the beer was flavoured with wormwood. It may be appropriate here to squash the myth that the English drink warm beer. This is not the case, beer being kept for the most part in a cool cellar. It has been called warm because it is not chilled as in most other countries. English beer is an acquired taste but should be persevered with. As I can personally testify, it has a unique, delicious flavour unequalled anywhere else in the world.

Cow or ox tongue pickled in vinegar, along with Stilton cheese, served with a spoon so the maggots could not escape, were eaten along with the copious amounts of beer or cider. This was brought from Devon and often mixed with turnips and sold as a kind of claret.

Tottenham Court Road was the place to be for any members of the drinking club on the sixteenth of October, 1814, as a tidal wave of beer swept through the streets. This followed the explosion of a container spilling over one million pints into the streets and destroying several houses. The accident being heard over five miles away, several people were suffocated in the rush to get at the ale.

There were many sharp practices effected by shopkeepers and traders. Flour was often mixed with chalk, sand with sugar, water with milk and much of the produce was well past its 'sell-by' date. Fruit was washed in filthy water and often barges that brought in vegetables took back sewage from the capital to use as manure on the vegetable farms.

48. Poultry and meat for sale.

49. *The dining room at the Cheshire Cheese, 1903.*

Milk was carried uncovered through the towns at risk to anything and everything thrown from the overlooking windows, it often standing about for days and going sour.

The upper classes were not too particular about what they ate as long as there was plenty of it and Samuel Johnson was reported as having consumed at one sitting; a leg of pork, veal pie with plums and sugar and salted beef. He rounded the meal off with plum pie and lobster sauce.

The poorer inhabitants also mixed sweet and savoury, wrapping the odd rare piece of meat into a baked pancake, the idea being to eat the outer casing to get to the delicacy on the inside. Early Christmas puddings and mincemeat both had meat in them, this being conserved by the sugar.

Life in the Victorian workhouse could only be tolerated with the help of large quantities of alcohol and whilst several thousand ate like pigs 'above-stairs' millions scavenged and made do with very poor food and as much alcohol as they could get hold of downstairs.

The shops became more specialised and started selling branded goods. Salted and tinned meats were imported from as early as 1847 but they did not as first make a great impression on the home market.

The butchers shops were not for the squeamish. The slaughterhouse stank and there was no humane way of killing the animals. The bullocks were pole-axed, hit just below the horn making an incision into the brain. A cane was then pushed in to break the spinal cord. A man was paid extra to clean the cesspool where the blood and rubbish went down.

The butchers were open until about eight o'clock weekdays but as late as midnight on Saturdays when the 'old girls' did their shopping. The poorer classes bought the odds and ends and some even bought pure fat with a little salt, while sausages were a treat made by a special 'gut man' who also produced haslets and filled the bladders with lard.

Fruit and vegetables were not overly popular amongst the Victorian working-class and they refused to allocate their scarce resources to buying them. There was a scare that tomatoes induced cancer. As in earlier days it was thought that the humble potato was responsible for flatulence and even leprosy.

There were experiments in freezing food as long ago as 1626. Francis Bacon, more noted for his writing and statesmanship, experimented in food preservation. He stuffed a chicken with fresh snow but could not continue his experiments, dying from a severe cold contracted in the pursuit of science.

Any goods no longer fit to be sold would be turned into ketchup or wine by an enterprising greengrocer's wife.

There was always a ready market for freshly poached game.

Both W.H. Davies and George Orwell spent some time experiencing the life of a tramp on London's streets but the most graphic account is that of Jack London in 'People of the Abyss,' published at the turn of the century.

He describes waiting in a queue for a 'spike' to open;

"Conversation was slack at first, standing there, till the man on one side of me and the man on the other side of me discovered that they had been in the smallpox hospital at the same time . . Their faces were badly pitted (though each assured the other that this was not so), and further they showed me in their hands and under the nails the smallpox 'seeds' still working out. Nay, one of them worked a seed out for me edification, and pop it went, right out of his flesh into the air. I tried to shrink up smaller inside my clothes, and I registered a fervent though silent hope that it had not popped on me.

At six o'clock the line moved up, and we were admitted in groups of three. Name, age occupation, place of birth, condition of destitution, and the previous night's 'doss', were taken with lightning-like rapidity by the superintendent; and as I turned I was startled by a man's thrusting into my hand something that felt like a brick, and shouting into my ear, 'any knives, matches, or tobacco.' 'No, sir,' I lied, as lied every man who entered. As we passed downstairs to the cellar I looked at the 'brick' in my hand, and saw that by doing violence to the language, it might be called 'bread'. By its weight and hardness it certainly must have been unleavened.

The place light was very dim down in the cellar, and before I knew it some other man had thrust a pannikin into my other hand. Then I stumbled on to a still darker room, where were benches and tables and men. The place smelled vilely, and the sombre gloom, and the mumble of voices from out of the obscurity, made it seem more like some anteroom to the infernal regions.

Most of the men were suffering from tired feet, and they prefaced the meal by removing their shoes and unbinding the filthy rags with which their feet were wrapped. This added to the general noisiness while it took away from the appetite . . .

. . . By seven o'clock we were called away to bathe and go to bed. We stripped our clothes, wrapping them up in our coats and buckling our belts about them, and deposited them in a heaped rack and on the floor — a beautiful scheme for the spread of vermin. Then, two by two, we entered the bathroom. There were two ordinary tubs, and this I know: the two men preceding had washed in that water, we washed in the same water, and it was not changed for the two men that followed us. This I know, but I am also certain that the twenty-two of us washed in the same water . . . Grunting, groaning, and snoring arose like the sounds emitted by some sea-monster, and several times afflicted by nightmare, one or other by his shrieks and yells, aroused the lot of us. Towards morning I was awakened by a rat or some similar animal on my breast. In the quick transition from sleep to waking, before I was completely myself, I raised a shout to wake the dead. At any rate I woke the living, and they cursed me roundly for my lack of manners.

At eight o'clock we went down into a cellar under the infirmary, where tea was brought to us, and the hospital scraps. These were heaped high on a huge platter in an indescribable mess — pieces of bread, chunks of grease and fat pork, the burnt skin from the outside of roasted joints, bones, in short, all the leavings from the fingers and the mouths of the sick suffering from all manner of diseases. Into this mess the men plunged their hands, digging, pawing, turning over, examining, rejecting, and scrambling for. It wasn't pretty. Pigs couldn't have done worse. But the poor devils were hungry, and they ate ravenously of the swill, and when they could eat no more they bundled what was left into their handkerchief and thrust it inside their shirts.''

50. Plea for any left-overs, c1869.

THE MOST INFAMOUS POACHERS OF ALL TIME

Ebenezer knew he was dying. The hefty prison sentence and spell in the workhouse had taken their toll and struggling from his bed he was determined to die a young man's death. Despite his age and condition he managed to pass through Hitchin on his last journey. By the moonlight he knew so well he made his way to his old poaching territory and birthplace.

The mind was willing but the flesh weak. About halfway home his legs gave out and he left the road crawling back to nature where he'd spent most of his 'working' life.

The body of Ebenezer Albert Fox, one of the most infamous poachers of all time was discovered in a woodland thicket three days later.

Ebenezer Albert and Albert Ebenezer Fox were born in 1857. They were identical twins who were never to grow above 5'2" though both were stocky, strong and blessed most of the time with a good nature. They had the healthy tan acquired by those who spend a great deal of time outdoors and were in most ways normal apart from their one obsession in life — poaching. If the Guinness Book of Records had existed then the two brothers would probably still hold the record of convictions with Ebenezer on eighty-two and Albert one hundred and eighteen. During their lifetime they were to lose over fifty guns of all varieties, hundreds of traps and snares and long lengths of silk and string netting, all confiscated by the authorities.

Both boys left school at eleven with an excellent knowledge of the countryside and the 'fruit' on offer. They were caught poaching for the first time at the age of fourteen but were let off after their solicitor suggested they were indulging in a misguided 'isolated' prank. The magistrates were not so lenient the next month with the boys being fined 10s.6d. Sometimes the Fox brothers paid the fines, at others they spent a week or two in the local gaols.

The brothers would hunt anything that moved and were good shots and accomplished poachers finding a ready market for their ware amongst the local tradesmen. In one month alone the brothers and their dog managed to net over one thousand rabbits.

As we have seen they were often tracked down themselves by angry gamekeepers but would come up with some original defences in court. They developed a hurt and resentful look whilst sentence was passed but took most convictions in good heart though they never intended to change their means of income. On one of the occasions Ebenezer was apprehended by a game-keeper, he managed to hide his gun and snare. At the magistrates court the Chairman of Hitchin bench opened;

"Alright Fox, I acknowledge you were without game or gun when arrested. But can you tell me why you were there, in a wood at dead of night, if not for an illegal purpose?"

Ebenezer kept a straight face as he replied; "I was there to meditate upon the Baptist hymn book."

Many in the courtoom could not control their laughter but with Ebenezer's practiced look of hurt he stared at the magistrate as he fumbled in his pockets before holding aloft the aforementioned book.

Like the Krays after them the Foxes were not slow at exploiting other peoples inability to tell them apart. It seemed sensible to poach alone and if caught to give the other brother's name and until the introduction of fingerprinting at the turn of the century they avoided many prosecutions using these tactics.

The twins were as cunning as their name implied and when one lady landowner promised Albert one pound a week and a brace of pheasant not to poach on her land he readily agreed. Ebenezer had the field to himself!

When Albert was fined £1 by a landowning magistrate he asked for twenty-four hours to pay. This request being granted he set off for the magistrate's land that night and had easily 'earned' his fine by the next day.

Albert was to discuss shooting with the Prince of Wales, later Edward VII when his car broke down on the way to Newmarket races. The two appeared to get on like a house on fire as they drank and swopped stories in a local pub.

The two brothers lived in rather a primitive home they built themselves. This gypsy-type hut was made exclusively from twigs, branches and turf and was known as Woodbine Cottage. They had become celebrities in the area and when referred to in the local press were called "those genial sporting gentlemen who are familiar figures in the local courts on Game Law summonses."

Ebenezer was not such a sporting gentleman as he got older and one day lost his cool with a gamekeeper. He was found guilty on a charge of G.B.H. and sentenced to ten years' imprisonment from which he was never fully to recover, deafness putting an end to his poaching days.

Albert kept on 'working' past retirement age and after his brother's death through exposure. He died at the age of eighty and both were to find immortality of a kind as they occupied a space on the wall of Scotland Yard's Black Museum, under the title — 'The most Infamous Poachers of all time."

51. *Albert Ebenezer and Ebenezer Albert Fox.*

MEASUREMENTS.			MEASUREMENTS.	
Head Length	18·7		Head Length	18·3
Head Breadth	15·5		Head Breadth	15·7
Left Mid. Finger	11·2		Left Mid. Finger	11·2
Left Cubit	43·6		Left Cubit	43·7
Left Foot	25·0		Left Foot	24·8
Face Breadth	14·17		Face Breadth	14·4
Height	5 ft. 2⅞ in.		Height	5 ft. 2⅝ in.

52. *The introduction of finger-printing has a great set-back for the Fox twins.*

HEALTH AND HYGIENE

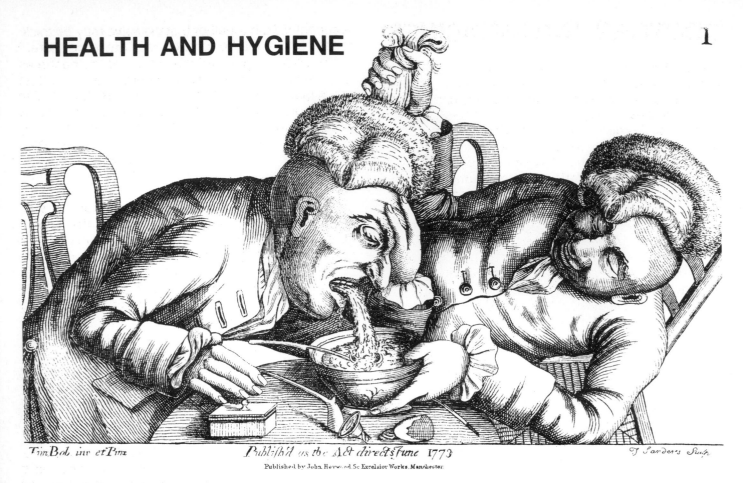

Tim Bob inv et Pinx

Publish'd as the Act directs June 1773

J Sanders Sculp

Published by John Heywood, Sc Excelsior Works, Manchester.

53. Man being sick.

For two hundred years after the Norman invasion the drinking water in London was of a high standard; 'They had in every street and lane of the city divers fayre wells and fresh springs'

By 1340 however the population had grown to 45,000 and it was the largest city in Britain, bringing about some of the first pollution problems. If you happened to be in a boat on the river Fleet it paid to keep an eye on the houses built over it as you stood a good chance of being soaked or soiled, though not through the weather. Latrines were hung over the river and ''each privie seat is filled with buttock''

William Atte-Wood was not the sort of person you would like to move in next door as he was prosecuted for causing ''great nuisance and discomfort to his neighbours by throwing out horrible filth on the highway, the stench of which is so odious that none of his neighbours can remain in the shops.''

For those who did not have the desirable river view other arrangements had to be made. A report by Erasmus in 1518 describes home interiors, and these were the wealthier classes: 'Floors are strewed with clay, and that covered with rushes which are now and then renewed, but not so as to disturb the foundation, which sometimes remains for twenty years nursing a collection of spittle, vomits, excrements of dogs and human beings, spilt beer and fishes bones and other filth that I need not mention.'

By Elizabethan times many householders were using cesspits below their houses this being encouraged by the government as it helped produce saltpetre which was used in the manufacture of gunpowder.

Toilet paper did not come onto the market until the 1860s but it was only for use by the wealthier classes. An account of the conditions in one of London's workhouses in 1866 shows the habit of wiping oneself had not yet caught on. 'Waste paper for use at the water-closet is supplied in but very few workhouses. This appears to be really both a hardship to the inmates and a disgrace to the guardian; and has led in numberless instances to the use of old towels, dusters and dishcloths, which were thrown down the water-closet and in not a few instances stopped them up. It was however stated — and it certainly applies too much to country populations — that a very large proportion of the poor do not use waste paper in their homes and do not therefore notice the necessity for it.'

When the Romans left Britain it seemed they took the habit of bathing with them. In Norman times, soap, such as it was, was made from scraps of meat-fat and an alkaline from wood ash. These were boiled together and the water softened by the addition of human urine which had been stored until it was suitably strong.

It seemed standards had improved somewhat by Elizabethan times as one courtier wrote of the Queen: 'She doth bathe herself once a month whether she require it or not.'

The manufacture of soap improved over the centuries but when a soap tax was levied between 1712 and 1853 many people chose to go without and court life in the eighteenth century consisted of 'dice, dancing, crowding, sweating and stinking in abundance.'

To offset their smell the rich bought expensive perfumes, often using them to excess.

DOCTORS AND MEDICINES

The capital's earliest 'Doctors' had a great belief in magic and spells. Charms were hung around patients' necks and secret magic potions concocted. Astrology was as important as the magic and the medical profession consulted the stars for the best time to implement their treatment.

Early enemas were effected with a pigs bladder and a tube. If you were suffering from consumption there is a good chance you would be given a 'prescription' containing hog-lice. For those suffering from quinsy (severe inflammation of the tonsils and throat) there was a new ointment on the market and upon consulting the list of ingredients you would find, amongst others; a fat cat, the grease of a hedgehog and the fat of a bear.

The Anglo-Saxons went to extraordinary lengths to ensure that their offspring would be male. It would not be unusual for the parents to take;

"A hare's uterus, dried and cut into slices or rubbed into a drink. Let them both drink it. If the wife alone drinks it then she will bear a hermaphrodite."

The early doctors also believed in less complicated cures and a highly recommended remedy for falling sickness was to drink spring water from the skull of a murdered man. Even medieval man suffered from headaches but he could not just reach for the aspirin. Instead he would follow these instructions;

"Take a vessel full of leaves of green rue, and a spoonful of mustard seed, and the white of an egg, a spoonful. Rub together that the salve may be thick. Smear with a feather on the side that is not sore."

The Middle Ages had their share of toothache as well, and as today in medicine there was more than one school of thought as to how to cure illness. The more radical thought that toothache was caused by worms eating away at the tooth from the inside. They advocated using candles to heat the teeth to force the worms out. The 'natural' school of thought recommended walking three times around a church yard.

The most dreaded disease in early London was leprosy. There were leper colonies in the capital between the tenth and fifteenth centuries, their numbers varying enormously, depending upon the other conditions of the time. In what is now St. James's Park there used to be a colony where lepers kept their hogs, though under no circumstances were they allowed into the City of London.

The lepers endured a most awful life of deprivation, not even being allowed to walk downwind of an unaffected person lest they pass on their illness.

Everywhere they went they had to ring a bell and beat wooden clappers to warn of their approach and food would be thrown to them from a distance. They were obliged to sport a distintive cloak and hood with the females wearing a thick veil. Various cures were attempted including plastering, bleeding and consuming a concoction made from leeks and boiled adders, all to no avail. In the end the lepers either died from starvation or during the Black Death.

54.   *A mercury cure for venereal disease, c1500.*

55. *An early enema.*

Over half the population of London were wiped out in what was probably the world's most virulent pandemic. The Black Death was so named because of the black patches which formed on the skin. The other symptoms included swellings in the groin or armpits. It was a very fast worker, sometimes taking less than twenty-four hours from the first signs to an early grave. 'How many valiant men, how many fair ladies breakfasted with their kinsfolk and that same night supped with their ancestors in the other world?'

It has been estimated that the Black Death killed one third of the entire population of England. London suffered so badly because the capital already had pollution problems, being the largest city in the land.

There were many more outbreaks of pox and flukes which were to have a devastating effect on the inhabitants of the capital. At the very start of the Tudor period in 1485 sweating sickness caused the death of two Lord Mayors and four Aldermen in one week. It would begin with shivering and a violent fever followed by headache, lethargy, abdominal pain and profuse perspiration — hence its name. The whole process lasted about twenty-four hours and your fate was determined in this time — most died.

The stench is decscribed in a written report from the time; 'A grete swety & stynkyng, with redness of the face and body, and a contynued thirst, with a grete hete and hedeche because of the fumes and venoms.'

The causes of sweating sickness which was often to return to London in the 1500s, though only in summer, were thought to be an excess of meat in the diet and the lack of fresh vegetables, the drinking of cider, the excess of clothing especially thick dirty caps worn by men. Others put down the cause to the dirty personal habits of Londoners and the scarcity of soap.

In the sixteenth and seventeenth centuries the following ingredients were to be found in the various medicines and ointments used in the fight against poor health: Powdered human skull, the blood of weasels, balsam of bats, snails mashed with bay salt, human urine and woodlice grained with sugar and nutmeg, fishes' eyes, dung tea, crushed worms and stewed owls. The ground-up dust from ancient Egyptian mummies changed hands at extortionate rates as it was deemed to be beneficial to health until the seventeeth century. The breath of young girls was also in great demand and old men wishing to prolong their lives would bribe girls to breathe invigorating vapours into their faces.

A typical seventeenth century remedy for the cure of malaria is taken from 'The New London Dispensary' by Salmon published in 1682.

"To cure quartans and gout, take the hair and nails of the patient, cut them small, and either give them to the birds in a roasted egg or put them in a hole in an oak tree or a plane tree. Stop up the hole with a peg of the same tree."

Strange though it may seem some cures actually worked. In the eighteenth century a prominent figure suffering from a stye rubbed it with the tail of a black cat and the swelling went down, though this is not recommended today. An entire boiled chicken consumed with five quarts of small beer was said to have cured dropsy, though after the consumption of alcohol it is quite possible that the patient forgot his illness.

Speaking of forgetfulness there was in Fleet Street or was it St. Paul's church a concoction on sale which cured loss of memory. There was no shortage of what we would today call quacks though many of these people were held in very high esteem and made huge fortunes selling their expertise.

By the year 1795 John Lettsom was reported to have attended to 82,000 patients, wearing out three horses a day on his rounds, a record unlikely to be surpassed in the famous Guinness book. He was a man not without a pragmatic outlook and rather black humour as he wrote of himself;

> When any sick to me apply
> I physichs, bleeds and sweat's 'em;
> If after that they choose to die,
> What's that to me, I lettsom.

James Graham set up a temple of health in Pall Mall in 1780. The house walls were decorated with 'walking sticks, ear trumpets, visual glasses, crutches etc left as most honourable trophies by deaf, weak, paralytic and emaciated persons, cripples etc who being cured had no longer need of such assistance.'

The rest of the house was sumptuously furnished and fitted with immense mirrors, globes of glass and dragons breathing flames. There was also a bed hired out for £100 per night to childless couples. The bed was one of the most luxurious ever manufactured and even played music to relax the prospective parents enjoying their stint in between the expensive sheets.

It's hard to find that kind of service these days though the prices are already with us. It is thought that Graham used Emma Lyon, the future Lady Hamilton, as a model posing as the Goddess of Health . Graham was way ahead of his time in the advertising stakes. Not only did he employ the top models of the day he also introduced a unique marketing policy. He would advertise in leaflets which were distributed by extremely tall, immaculately dressed servants delivering handbills to the doors of prospective customers. Graham became a very rich man but there is a fine dividing line between genius and lunatic and he eventually died penniless in an asylum.

Joshua 'Spot' Ward — he was called Spot because of a birthmark on his face — became famous thanks to the enormous quantities of drops and pills he sold. He was one of the king's favourites and was granted the rare privilege of being allowed to drive his carriage through St James's Park. 'Crazy' Sally Mopp was a bonesetter who drove to London twice a week in a magnificent coach and four with liveried attendants to consult at the Grecian Coffee House. She was another character centuries ahead of her time and knew the value of hype. Once again she made a lot of money before dying in obscurity. Although it got

56. *Re-construction of an operation before anaesthetics. (A Gordon Fraser Card)*

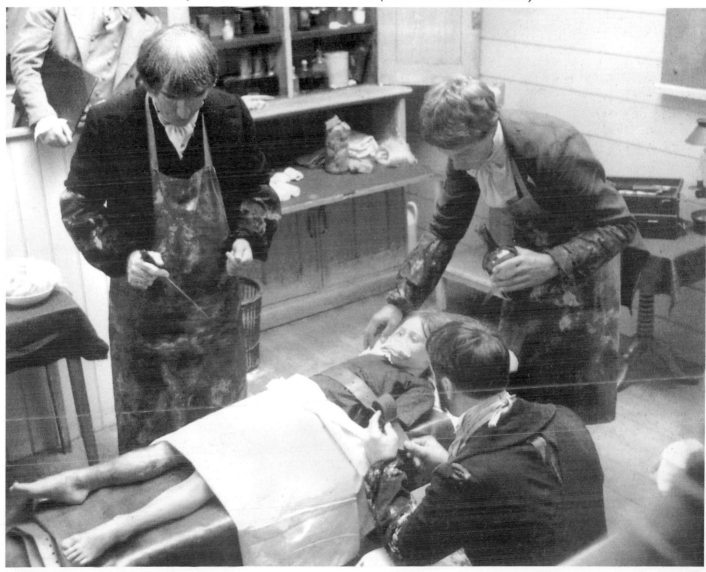

off to a slow start, the nineteenth century was to see the breakthrough in medical treatment. Most illnesses until that time had been treated with herbs, spices, pills, spells, prayer, diet, bleeding or crude surgery. The medical profession was forever experimenting and in 1773 John Hunter inoculated himself to see whether syphilis and gonorrhoea were the same disease. He was buried in Westminster Abbey.

Hospitals in the eighteenth century were more like rest homes and the nurses looked upon as servants. Breakfast consisted of thin gruel; lunch 6oz of meat with no vegetables; dinner, a kind of broth washed down with two or three pints of beer. The whole diet was often supplemented from the nearby ginhouse.

The long wards were lined with beds whose mattresses were stuffed with straw or hair and more often than not infested with bugs. Nurses were often forced to 'live in' and housed in the attics or basements and as today, very much exploited. Very few had any qualifications with many being too old or feeble to lift the patients from their beds though they were rather adept at stealing the patients' food. The meagre pay was mostly spent on beer or gin.

There was a great interest in surgery in the early 1800s and amputations were the most common treatment for compound fractures. The patient was strapped to the kitchen table and hymns were sung to counteract the pain. The surgeon would wear an old blood stained coat and place a tray under the table to catch the laudable pus which dripped from the wound. It was in everybody's interest that the operation be carried out as swiftly as possible and there was nobody quicker than the larger than life figure of Robert Liston (1794-1847) who moved to London from his native Scotland. He was a tall, extremely powerful man and the darling of the Surgical Schools, a top box-office attraction.

It was said of him that when he operated the gleam of his knife was followed so swiftly by the sound of sawing as to make the two actions appear almost simultaneous.

His physical strength was such that he could amputate a thigh with only a single assistant to hold the limb. He would not use a tourniquet, controlling the blood vessels to a limb with one hand and carrying out the amputation with the other. During one operation Liston was faced with the problem of profuse bleeding which was emanating from a large blood vessel in the substance of an amputated leg. Without hesitating he seized the amputating knife and sliced a wedge of wood off the operating table and with the handle of the knife hammered it into the blood vessel. The haemorrhaging stopped and the patient recovered.

Liston was an extremely fast worker, it taking only two flashes of the straight knife and three strokes of the saw before the limb dropped to the sawdust below. Sometimes the obsession with speed had disastrous results. On one occasion Liston amputated a leg in two and a half minutes. When he stood back to admire his handiwork he noticed that he had also sawn off the patient's testicles.

57. Hospital ward — early 20th century.

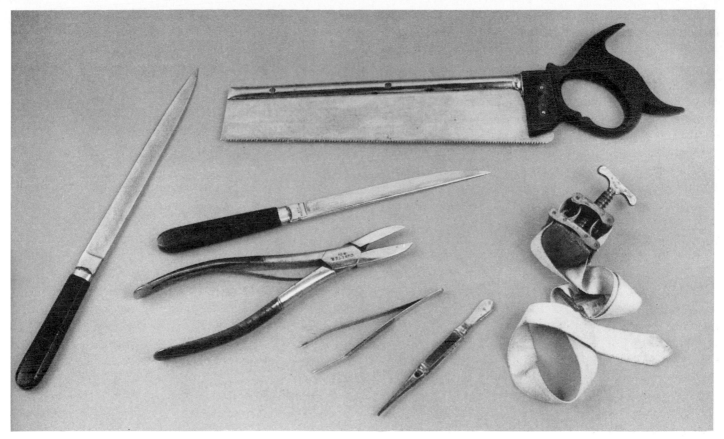

58. Surgeons tools early 19th century. (A Gordon Fraser Card)

He managed to perform another operation in an even shorter period of time but the patient died of gangrene. In his haste he also cut off the fingers of a young assistant who later died and he managed to slash through the coat and tails of a distinguished surgical spectator who so feared that his manhood had been relegated to the sawdust that he dropped dead from fright. This must be one of the few operations in history with a three hundred per cent mortality rate.

As many people owed their life to Liston as lost it. On another occasion a patient with a soft swelling on his neck had had it misdiagnosed as an abscess. Liston plunged the knife in and was immediately covered in arterial blood. He managed to close the wound with his broad thumb and stop the bleeding.

Later in his career Liston was one of the first surgeons to experiment with ether. He announced to the spectators at the operation; 'Gentlemen, we are going to try a yankee dodge to make men insensible'

The patient was anaesthetized and the leg off in twenty eight seconds and the wound sewn up. A few moments later the patient sat up and asked;

"When are you going to begin?"

Upon being shown the amputated stump of his thigh he lay back whimpering.

Liston turned to the audience and proclaimed;

"This, this yankee dodge, gentlemen, beats mesmerism hollow."

Despite the growing use of anaesthetics in the second half of the nineteenth century surgery was still in its infancy. Barton describes an operation about one hundred years ago.

"Close up to the left hand door in the corner you see a small wash basin about the size of a large soup plate, in which the surgeons washed their hands after — sometimes even before — operating. Alongside the basin is a row of pegs from which hang the operating coats of the staff. These were mostly old frock coats, stiff and stinking with pus and blood. The more advanced however, after removing their coats would put on a grocer's bib and apron of some non-absorbent stuff.

On entering the theatre to operate, the surgeon would take off his coat and don his 'operating coat' rolling up his sleeves and turning up the collar over his white linen, to save this from some errant vessel's attention. The area was railed off, and only the staff or visiting outsiders were permitted entrance during operations. Liston's table stood in the centre of the arena with its head towards the sliding doors. Patients were wheeled or walked into a side room which opened to it under the stairs. Here they were anaesthetized and wheeled into the theatre where they were lifted onto the table.

The table was covered with a blanket, over this was a large sheet of brown oil cloth coming well down over the blanket. Beneath the table may be seen a wooden box about 18"x12"x4" deep filled with sawdust. This box can be kicked by the surgeon's foot to any place where most blood is running in little gutters off the oil cloth. As the sawdust becomes unable to absorb any more and is converted into a bloody porridge, one hears the surgeon call "More sawdust, Holder," when a fresh boxful is placed under the table."

Several seemingly strange cures or superstitions have lasted into the twentieth century. A novel cure for rheumatism and chest complaints was introduced from Belgium during the First World War, the sufferer being recommended to wear a cat skin. One London superstition that died out as the other was being introduced concerns whooping cough. As a cure a sandwich should be made from hair cut at the back of a child's head. It should then be given to the first passing dog, the theory being that the unfortunate canine picks up the disease. An early example of the hair of the dog?

Because of the prohibitive expense of doctors in the first half of the century, many Londoners improvised their own cures. The most common were for coughs and colds where it was thought that onions were most beneficial. One remedy recommends soaking an onion in brown sugar and drinking the liquid. Tea made from fresh garlic was the cure for bad chests though you might find yourself losing visitors. It might be cheaper to call the doctor than put into practice the popular cure for warts. Raw beef was to be placed over the unwanted growth and then buried. When the beef has rotted the wart should also disappear. Two other cures, a little cheaper this time; sell the warts to somebody or lick them every night before going to sleep.

If you wanted your baby to have curly hair wipe its head with a wet nappy. One remedy that is still touted today is that a cow licking the head can cure baldness!

Tragical History Tours accepts no responsibility if for one reason or another these cures do not work.

Tooth pulling was not considered a skilled profession and was carried out as a sideline by varied other workers including cobblers, blacksmiths and hairdressers, a form of pliers being the most common tool.

Sometimes a pulled tooth was replaced by another from a healthy person's jaw and tooth extractors had such signs as 'money given for live teeth' outside their premises. It was not uncommon to see the poor and children leave these premises without a tooth left in their head. On other occasions dogs, goats, baboons and sheep's teeth were transplanted to human jaws, and there was a ready market for sets procured by the grave-robbers. After wars teeth, both artificial and real, were collected by the thousand from the corpses.

These animal and false teeth often led to bad breath and ladies used their fans either to wave it away or prevent it from being noticed by acquaintances. In earlier days toothpicks were used and teeth rubbed with a cloth or sponge, brushes being introduced in the mid-nineteenth century.

There were various sets of false teeth to suit every price range but the cheap celluloid ones did not stay on the market for long because if their owner was a smoker his whole mouth might have gone up in flames.

An indication as to medical thinking in the early years of this century may be gleaned from interviews in the Age Exchange publication "Can We Afford the Doctor?"

"The thick yellow fog that we used to have, really thick yellow. You couldn't see your hand in front of you, literally. This was killing to anyone with chest trouble and I used to spend a lot of time in bed having steam kettles and old fashioned remedies. I had very long, very black glossy hair and this old doctor told my mother once that the hair was taking all the strength from my body and I had to have it cut. So she took me straight round to the barbers and I had my hair cut really short. When I got home my father went really mad because he really loved this hair, and that's the sort of doctor he was, really old fashioned, and I would have thought totally useless really.

There were fever boats somewhere round about Woolwich. There were half a dozen as far as I can remember and they were moored off the shore. People had scarlet fever, diptheria, things like that. I gathered from what my mother said that they were short of barges. Mum worked there for some time. She had to stay there for some months at a time and live on board. Apparently she caught something. I don't know what it was — scarlet fever I think — and after she'd been nursed there on the boat she had to leave because they wouldn't have her back.

THE SPANISH LADY COMES TO LONDON

Londoners thought their visits to the cemeteries for premature deaths were over as the 'War to End Wars' drew to a close in 1918. Few people probably noticed the message received by Reuters from Spain: 'A strange form of Disease of Epidemic character has appeared in Madrid. The epidemic is of a mild nature, no deaths having been reported'

This 'mild epidemic' was soon to affect eight million in Spain alone before setting off on a world tour which would leave tens of millions dead in its wake. The 'Influenza' was brought to London via the port of Liverpool and Glasgow. To begin with the London hospitals were flummoxed and just directed the B.I.D.s (brought in dead) to the mortuary. The sheer number gave way to concern that was to border on panic and change the lives, some permanently, of the capital's inhabitants. The first signs were the onset of fever, followed by a cough, aches in the head, back and legs. Those who did not recover from these early symptoms would start to experience great difficulty

59. 'Anything else sir?'

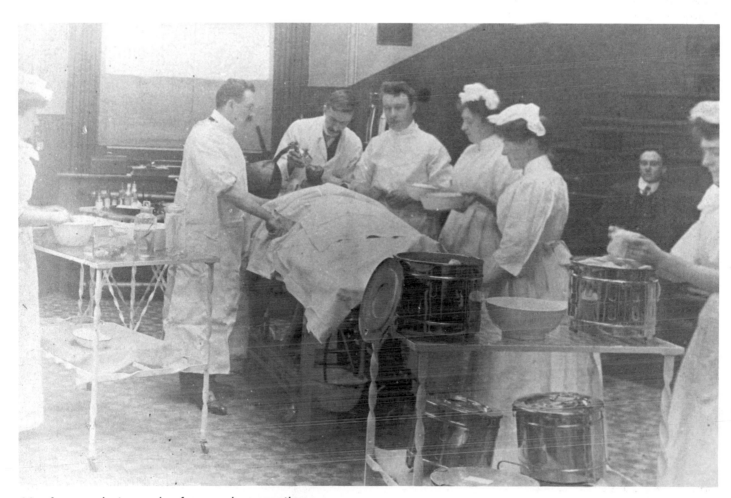

60. A rare photograph of an early operation.

with their lungs, many coughing up as much as two pints of yellow-green pus every day. At autopsies lungs upto six times their normal weight were often discovered. The victims' urine was also affected with quite often only ten ounces of blood-streaked water being passed daily as opposed to the normal three pints. The patient occasionally lapsed into a coma for three weeks, the middle-ear cavity becoming choked with pus and the eye-muscle paralysed.

The buses and streets were sprayed with disinfectant as the medical profession tried to get to grips with the greatest pandemic since the Black Death. Leonard Hill from London's Hospital Medical School urged that the entire population of Great Britain should sleep in the open air. Smoking in war plants was permitted for the first time as it was hoped this would act as a 'germicide'.

For the first time in the capital's public health records the death rate in the more prosperous areas of Westminster and Chelsea was as high as in the slums of the East End. For the week ending February 22 1919 there were 1,201 births and 2,645 deaths in London and attendance at funerals often made matters worse. Doctors were often passed on sets of keys when the whole family was laid up and he would be greeted with signs stating; 'Walk in — Don't knock — All in bed.'

Pregnant women were amongst the most vulnerable of the population and it has been estimated that about half of the deaths were in the 20-40 age group. One hundred boys who had been inoculated at Greenwich Royal Hospital School remained immune despite flu being rife in the area.

There are always those ready to take advantage of any turmoil and at St Marylebone's Police Court one man was charged with stealing a £20 car. He introduced a unique defence when he produced a doctor's certificate stating that the after-effects of flu 'had clouded his moral sense.'

At Hampstead Hospital a nurse reported for duty when perhaps she should have gone home after being treated with gas by her dentist. She was feeling drowsy before taking over the care of a flu victim whose chest contained two huge hollow needles. These were connected by rubber tubes to an oxygen cylinder as the man was unable to swallow or breath properly. The effects of the morning visit soon caused the nurse to drop off to sleep and she slumped forward onto the valve controlling the flow of oxygen. When the nurse finally came round the cylinder was empty and the man had taken on the appearance of a fully inflated balloon. The gas had been forced under the skin at pressure and a great deal had gotten into the patient's bloodstream. He was one of the luckier ones, eventually making a complete recovery. Altogether about 225,000 Britons were killed out of an estimated world total of over twenty-one million. It is thought that one half of the entire population of the world was attacked in one way or another. Like the Plague and Black Death it disappeared almost as suddenly as it appeared, though it was to return in future years in a much milder form.

Out-Patient Department, London Hospital.   London E.

61. Most patients took to their beds during this 'flu epidemic.

EDUCATION

62. One of the early 'ragged schools'.

Schooling is a process we have all been through, some enjoying their time, others indifferent and several looking upon the process as 'having their Education interrupted'. Whatever one may think of the process school pupils have changed very little over the centuries. In the 1200s the teachers at Westminster School were on the lookout for pupils who were grinning, chatting or laughing out loud. Making fun of those who could not properly read the psalms was another punishable offence and those who secretly hit their companions or answered each other back were not spared the rod.

It seems the boarders at Westminster were an unruly lot as there were strict rules against tearing or hiding bedclothes, throwing pillows or shoes around the dormitory and generally bringing about a state of disorder in the school.

Most of the teaching was of Latin grammar and the school day very long, often lasting from 6a.m. to 6p.m. Holidays were kept to a minimum. The Thatcherite idea of self support was very much in evidence with the pupils at St. Paul's school urinating into buckets

and having it sold to dyers and tanners. It was by these means that school funds were supplemented long before the days of the parent-teacher association. The boys would sit on long benches and listen to their masters as very few books were available.

Educational establishments did not change a great deal over the centuries with only a few privileged girls receiving an education. It has been estimated that in London in 1640 eighty per cent of London women were illiterate.

Those who were privileged made good scholars. Had Lady Jane Grey been born today she would surely be a member of MENSA, and Elizabeth I was extremely well read being able to speak Latin, French, Spanish and Italian and reading anything up to three hours of history per day.

Gradually more and more people began to realise the value of education and even the poor might receive a few lessons in church. With industrialisation and the drift to the cities the literacy rate actually went down and those who attended school in the middle of the nineteenth century were without their knowing

63. *Boys and girls were educated separately.*

64. *Boys learning craft.*

65. *Girls schools with very high walls*

66. *The sort of photo guaranteed to anger any present-day feminist teacher.*

being 'conditioned' to toil for the idle rich. Dr Kay-Shuttleworth innocently described the attitude to schools in 1846;

"Supervised by it's trusty teacher, surrounded by its playground wall, the school was to raise a new race of working people — respectful, cheerful, hard-working, loyal, pacific and religious."

Well-to-do girls were taught 'drawing room' skills such as piano playing, dancing and embroidery the main aim of which was to attract a husband. They were not encouraged to use their minds and would often flee into unhappy marriages to escape the insipid uselessness of their lives.

If we consider the home conditions in the middle of the nineteenth century we can see why there was a clamour to get children out of the homes and into schools. Dr Greenhow reported in 1861; 'Mothers employed in factories are, save during the dinner-hour, absent from home all day long, and the care of their infants during their absence is entrusted either to young children, to hired nurse girls sometimes not more than 8 or 10 years of age, or perhaps more commonly to elderly women, who eke out a living by taking infants to nurse. Young girls, aged 7 or 8 are frequently removed from school for the purpose of taking charge of younger children while the mother is absent at work, and are sometimes said to return, on the death of the child, evidently rather pleased that this event has released them from their toil . . .

Children who are healthy at birth rapidly dwindle under this system of mis-management, fall into bad health, and become uneasy, restless and fractious. To remedy the illness caused by mis-management, various domestic medicines are administered such as Godfrey's cordial, or laudanum. Wine, gin, peppermint and other stimulants are likewise often given, for the purpose, as alleged, of relieving flatulence, their actual effect being, however, rather to stupefy the child . . ."

Ragged schools under the supervision of concerned individuals such as Dr Barnardo began to mushroom throughout London in the 1870s. They attempted to provide a basic education for the Capital's poorest children. Evening classes and Sunday school tried to cater for the older factory workers and those who for one reason or another could not attend daytime classes.

The workers in these schools were horrified at the state of neglect and realised they had to look after their physical needs before effective education could take place. The half-starved children received one hot dinner a week which consisted of 'Irish stew, a good nutritious soup or of a meat cooked in some other way, with a plentiful supply of vegetables.'

By 1888 free breakfasts and dinners were provided in the winter months as Barnardo said of his pupils 'They know what it is to have no fire in the grate and no bread in the cupboard; and we find in many cases that food is more essential to the boys and girls than education.'

State education became compulsory in 1880 but there were difficulties in enforcing attendance. Many of the older girls would be absent on wash day and for much longer periods after the birth of a baby brother or sister. These 'little mothers' were often as young as seven or eight. In an 1897 report on attendance it was noted;

"During the summer months there is a large exodus from the neighbourhood for the hop and fruit-picking seasons. Not a few of the children also belong to the families of hawkers, wandering showmen, and of canal boatmen . . . The percentage of attendances, therefore, sometimes falls below fifty! Not merely do children who are so much absent lose the benefits of education, but it is a matter of extreme difficulty to maintain discipline over them when they do return."

Progress in health care and education was slow. In a survey towards the end of the century only one hundred and thirty seven children out of one thousand had 'sound dentition' with similar figures relating to eyesight and hearing. Many children worked part-time and possibly over 50% over ten years of age had jobs. It was still legal for children to be allowed into pubs where bowls of sweets were provided whilst their parents drank. There were no laws against children themselves drinking and if they fancied a flutter on the three thirty at Newmarket or a Capstan full strength nobody could stop them. In 1900 the infant mortality rate was 163 for every thousand births and for those that survived one in four did not reach their fifth birthday, whooping cough being the cause of almost half the deaths.

With the very unstable life in the overpopulated capital there was an increasing demand for orphanages, children's homes and reformatories. Here the regimes were extremely strict. In a reformatory in Fulham children had their hair shaved and would often be punched by the orderly. The children were not allowed to talk all night and after being roused at six o'clock would drill for two hours before their two slices and tea for breakfast.

The regime at orphanages was not a great deal more relaxed, with 'mothers' appearing in the dormitories at night to check whether the children were sleeping with their legs straight or bent — the 'bent' ones getting the rod.

Due to malnutrition many boys were deemed unfit for service in the forces and maybe for no other reason than this school dinners were introduced in 1906 and health inspectors a year later. As is the case today teachers were expected to live on a pittance and baths were not installed at a teacher training college so that teachers would not get a taste for a luxury they would not later be able to afford. Very few of the female teachers married and the rod was certainly not spared in the classroom. Probably the best way to get a picture of what life was like in the capital's schools is to read the accounts of those who went through the system . . .

67. 'Sit up straight and look at the camera.'

The following extracts are reprinted from the excellent Age Exchange Publication 'GOOD MORNING CHILDREN' and capture the spirit of the schools in the early part of the twentieth century.

"Once gathered in the classroom, there was the handkerchief drill. We were asked to produce our handkerchiefs (usually tucked up our knicker legs, or even pinned to our chests). Heaven help you if you had forgotten it! Some children might produce a rather soiled piece of rag, and I can remember the scathing comments of the teachers. Then we all had to give our noses a good blow, following which there were deep breathing exercises. All designed to clear our heads for the day's work!"
MARGARET KIPPIN

"I don't remember whether we had handkerchiefs or a piece of the old sheet or something like that. And whether we used to use it for our nose or not I don't know, but we used to wrap our old gobstopper up in it — you only ever used half of it you see and the bell's gone and you'd go to class, mustn't eat in class so you wrap it up till next time.
BILL WELCH

School lavatories were always situated out in the school yard, a good distance from the actual school. If it was raining, well, you got soaked through as you ran there and back.

The loos themselves were very primitive. They were housed in a low-lying brick building. The bricks were white-washed inside and out. The roof was corrugated iron and it was noisy when the rain pattered down. The loos were very small pans with wooden seats. There was no paper, but if you needed some you could usually find some pages of someone's exercise book, maybe even your own. Sometimes there would be comics. The door had a big gap top and bottom and just had an iron latch. There were no washing facilities at all.

Hardly anyone shut the doors, for loos were jolly good meeting places. We swopped exam or class questions, recited poetry, swopped jokes and we swopped comics and marbles. We arranged meeting places and generally gossiped. If my friends were sitting on the loo very often I would do a tap dance for them. A kind of entertainment as they sat. The loo wall was a jolly good wall for doing "hand-stands". We would tuck our tunics up the legs of our navy blue drawers, and with hands and heads down our legs would be up against the wall. We'd stay like that for ages. Yes, school loos were interesting places.
MILLY GARDNER

Once I was sent out of the room to another teacher. The whole lesson in that room stopped whilst that teacher said, "Yes what do you want?" He probably knew anyway. You said, "Oh Mr Ward I've been sent to you to get the cane." And all his class would prick up their ears and you'd have to say what you'd had the cane for. "I flicked paper across the room instead of listening to history." "Ah, yes, all right, fetch the cane for me then", and you had to stand in front of his class, so you had a feeling of humiliation, because there might have been some of your friends, there might even be your brother in that class, who's sure to tell your mother when you get home, that you've had the cane, so you get another one as well.
DOROTHY BARTON

TRAFFIC

In 1811 London was the first city in the world to record a population of over one million. With rapid expansion it kept poll position until 1957 when it was overtaken by Tokyo. England was therefore the first country to have to sort out the traffic jams and communications problems presented by such a density of population. Many people were opposed to the expansion of the railways and the Duke of Wellington thought a French army might arrive unannounced by train!

There was great concern amongst the local population when it was learned that the Woolwich to London train would travel as fast as eighteen miles per hour. In the early days passengers were trying to jump on or off the trains, many to retrieve their hats and in a typical year five people would be run over whilst lying on the track, either drunk or asleep. Nothing stood in the way of progress and altogether 56,000 people had to abandon their homes in London to make way for the railway lines between 1853 and 1883.

By 1845 the streets were choked with people, carts and animals being driven to market. When the idea of an underground was first proposed there were many objections as the concept was deemed to be contrary to the laws of God.

The first underground pulling open coaches left Baker Street in 1863. The Inner Circle line was completed in 1864 and was the first underground network in the world. Surprisingly it was not tunnelled but constructed by a cut and cover technique and the platforms were lit partly by natural light through a series of shafts. Since those days millions have travelled on the network and have left behind a strange assortment of articles including a stuffed gorilla, a box of glass eyes and bag of human bones.

When the first escalator was installed at an underground station the railway had to engage a man with a wooden leg to go up and down it all day to dispel fears amongst the travellers.

There were severe congestion problems with cars even at the turn of the century and London's first multi-storey car park was opened near Piccadilly Circus in 1901. The seven-floored building had a hydraulic lift capable of raising a three ton lorry to the top floor.

Colonel Pierpoint had trouble crossing St. James's Street to get to his club. He set about remedying this problem by installing London's first traffic island in 1864. He so admired his handywork that he was wont to gaze behind at it whilst crossing the road. He was knocked down by a cab.

68. Charing Cross Station 1890s.

LUDGATE HILL & CIRCUS FROM FLEET STREET. 4523.

69. *Fleet Street and Ludgate Circus, 1897.*

THE WOMEN'S MOVEMENT

London was the centre for one of the most fervent and original struggles the country and indeed the world has ever witnessed. Throughout the capital's history women had been surpressed and exploited but around the turn of the century they decided to take the law, that made by man, into their own hands and begin their struggle for equality in earnest.

For hundreds of years women had been deprived of education. James I refused to allow his daughter to learn Latin justifying his decision by stating; 'To make women learned and foxes tame has the same effect; to make them more cunning.'

Women were not allowed to own anything and the few who did manage to receive some form of education were often tormented and ridiculed by their male counterparts. Female writers were commonly known as petticoat-authors and mercilessly attacked for encroaching on a male domain.

"Alas! a woman who attempts the pen,
such an intruder on the rights of men."

In the nineteenth century unmarried women were considered the lowest of the low and forced into a dull life as servants in large households with long hours and precious little free time. Many of these servants took to a life of prostitution or employment in work houses and factories. It was the exploitation of female workers at The Bryant and May match factory in 1888 that led to one of the first working class boycotts of products and solidarity amongst female workers, many of whom were suffering from phossy-jaw due to their working conditions. For those who married, life was often one long round of baby-bearing and minding along with the daily drudge of trying to make ends meet. Infant mortality was high and the awful conditions took their toll on the women, many of them ageing before their time.

Even at the start of this century there was no place in the professions such as medicine or law for women and there were restrictions on the rights of inheritance and the rights to own property. Women were tolerated as teachers and nannies but were expected to remain celibate and behave as if they had taken vows of chastity. The Queen of all hypocrites, Victoria, even suggested that those agitating for reform should be whipped.

70. A Suffragette demonstrating in Whitehall.

71. *The arrest of Mrs. Pankhurst, 1914, while trying to present a petition to King George V at Buckingham Palace. The arresting officer died a fortnight later.*

72. *The campaign was responsible for some of the largest demonstrations ever witnessed in the capital.*

The movement for change began to gather momentum in the years leading up to the First World War. Women were told that they could not have the vote for such patronising reasons as; they were incapable of rational thought; too weak and frail to take on the burden of decision and thought to be too incapacitated by childbirth to bother with politics. It was much better for all those concerned that men should make decisions with the best interests of women at heart.

Women's pressure groups began to grow and when few people took notice of them they engaged in most original campaigns to promote their case. Faced with an unsympathetic House of Commons made up entirely of men they sought to gain maximum publicity, be it sympathetic or otherwise. The Chancellor of the Exchequor Asquith was one of the most outspoken members against the women's movement and while canvassing at elections he was followed around by women ringing bells and smacking any policemen present around the face. A Miss New chained herself to the railings in Downing Street and shouted "Votes for Women!" into the assembled cabinet. Miss Matters chartered a balloon and flew across the Capital dropping leaflets. Some women managed to get themselves addressed as a 'human letter' and sent to Downing Street but despite the 'letter' being recorded they were denied access. Women would pop up in the most unlikely of places to support their cause, one even hiding in the organ at the Albert Hall. Once the audience was assembled she jumped out shouting "Votes for women!"

By 1908 the capital was witnessing some of the largest demonstrations ever seen, with The Times estimating the crowd at one of the rallies to be half a million strong. The women were still no closer to attaining their goals so more drastic action had to be taken to take on the men in Downing Street. Pictures at the National Gallery were slashed, plants were wrecked in Kew Gardens and there were arson attacks with a refreshment kiosk in Kew Gardens being burned down. Later in the campaign there were to be bombings but a new tactic was becoming more and more popular — that of women deliberately seeking terms of imprisonment. This was often done by smashing shop windows with hammers in the centre of London. Constance Lytton described the procedure in her account of those years 'Prisons and Prisoners'. 'As soon as the Deputation had passed, the clock of Big Ben began striking eight. I said, "I can wait no longer," and I turned and smashed the glass of two doors and one window. I raised my arms and did it deliberately, so that everyone in the street could see. Miss Lawless smashed the windows to my right. We were going down the steps and I was afraid no policeman had been near, when two came over the way. All was peaceable and friendly. My policeman said to me with a smile, "I'll take you this way see,"

ii.—SUPPLEMENT TO THE ILLUSTRATED LONDON NEWS, Aug. 7, 1909.—ii

THE SCENE OF THE SUFFRAGETTES' "MARTYRDOM": HOLLOWAY PRISON—THE LIFE WITHIN ITS WALLS.

Photographs Specially Taken for "The Illustrated London News" by Reinhold Thiele.

1. FOOD FOR THE PRISONERS: A CORNER OF THE MEAT-STORES.
2. THE PRISONER'S DAILY RATIONS—BREAKFAST: ONE PINT OF GRUEL AND A SIX-OUNCE BROWN ROLL; DINNER: SIX OUNCES OF POTATOES, A SIX-OUNCE BROWN ROLL, TEN OUNCES OF BEANS, AND TWO OUNCES OF FAT BACON; SUPPER: ONE PINT OF GRUEL AND A SIX-OUNCE BROWN ROLL.
3. FOOD FOR THE PRISONERS: A CORNER OF THE STORE-ROOM.
4. HOW THE PRISONER MAY BE WATCHED: THE INTERIOR OF A CELL SHOWING THE SPY-HOLE FOR WARDRESSES IN THE DOOR, AND THE SHELF AND STOOL USED BY THE PRISONER AT MEAL-TIMES.
5. THE THRESHOLD OF LIFE UNDER RESTRAINT: THE RECEPTION-CELLS, IN WHICH PRISONERS SIT WHILE AWAITING THEIR TURN TO BATHE AND DRESS IN PRISON CLOTHES BEFORE BEING TAKEN TO THEIR PERMANENT CELLS.
6. FOOD FOR THE PRISONERS: A CORNER OF THE STORE-ROOM.

7. THE BATH-ROOM, WHICH WEARS A DREADED LIFE: THE RECEPTION ROOM.
8. WHERE THE PRISONERS' MEALS ARE PREPARED: A KITCHEN.
9. A LARGE BOILER FULL OF GRUEL.
10. ONE OF THE BATH-ROOMS.
11. A LARGE BOILER FULL OF GRUEL.
12. INDUSTRY IN THE PRISON: A ROOM IN WHICH BEAD BLINDS ARE MADE.

At the police station "we were put four or five together in a cell. The door was left open, and a wardress asked respectfully if she might search us. We said "Yes, most certainly", and began to deliver up our stones. The wardress's face was all kindness and no sooner had the policeman gone away from the door than she burst out with; "Oh! you ladies, I'd be with you tomorrow if it weren't for my child. I am a widow with one child. If only those politicians knew what that meant! They can talk fine about the widow, but when it comes to her earning a livelihood they don't help her."

On other occasions the prisoners were not so well treated, especially those who went on hunger strike.

This tactic was employed when suffragettes were refused political status in prison. Miss Wallace Dunlop was one of many who refused food in 1909;

"I threw a fried fish, four slices of bread, three bananas and a cup of hot milk out of my window on Tuesday, that being the only day I felt really hungry. They threatened all the time to pump milk through my nostrils but never did. They kept my table covered with food, which I never touched. I only drank water. My pulse was felt many times in the day and I laughed at them all the time, telling them I would show them the stuff a suffragette was made of; and that they would have to put me in the first division or release me."

Ninety-one hours later she was freed.

The government did not want to run the risk of having the deaths of martyrs on their hands and forced feeding was introduced to London prisons to alleviate their problem. The following two descriptions are some of many handed down by those who had to undergo this de-humanising and painful procedure:

"I was raised into a sitting position, and the tube about two foot long was produced. My mouth was prized open with what felt like a steel instrument, and then I felt them feeling for the proper passage. All the time I was held down by four or five wardresses. I felt a choking sensation and what I judged to be a cork gag was placed between my teeth to keep my mouth open. It was a horrible feeling altogether. I experienced great sickness, especially when the tube was being withdrawn."

On other occasions a nasal tube was used. Constance Lytton describes what happened to Miss Richardson.

"It took eight wardresses and one man to overcome her. On two occasions it was said; "Twist her arms — the only way to unlock them." They held her feet by pressing in the hollow of her ankles. Occasionally the doctor pressed her in the chest to hold her down. He announced that he was going to use the stomach tube. As he could not get through her teeth, he put his fingers to the extremity of her jaw, and with his finger-nail deliberately cut her gum and cheek until her mouth was bleeding badly. He then inserted the gag and stomach tube, but she was so choked by the experience process that he stopped the feeding, and said he would return to the nasal tube."

The government later changed their tactics to what was to become known as the cat and mouse act, releasing and then re-arresting prisoners a few days later.

By the year 1913 attitudes on both sides were hardening. There were reports of arson attacks from all over the country and bombs were reported to have been found in St. Paul's. One headline ran 'London is locked up'. It was against this background that Emily Wilding Davison was to make the ultimate sacrifice. On Derby Day at Tattenham Corner she ran out, Union Jack in hand, in front of the King's horse. The horse swerved throwing the jockey and Emily was caught up in the melee on the ground. The horse and jockey recovered and Emily died from her injuries four days later. Thousands turned out for the funeral when the procession made its way from Victoria to King's Cross. The mourners were dignified — lined up according to their profession with embroidered banners. They were dressed in black, purple, white and green and the spectacle along with the growing support from prominent figures, including many men, must have worried the government.

With 1914 came war and in 1918 after many women showed they could do 'men's' work as well if not better than those fighting the most senseless of wars overseas, the vote was granted to women over the age of thirty with full universal suffrage ten years later.

FORCIBLE FEEDING THROUGH THE NOSE OF WOMEN SUFFRAGIST PRISONERS,

Pronounced as dangerous by many Leading Members of the Medical Profession.

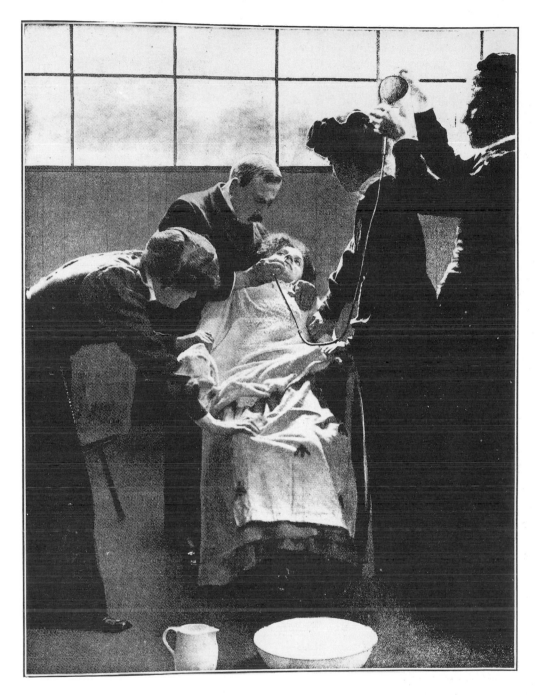

MISS SYLVIA PANKHURST, in a letter to the "Standard," dated April 25, states : "Lady Constance Lytton, when imprisoned as Jane Warton in Walton Goal, Liverpool, was forcibly fed without her heart having been tested. The doctor sat upon her knees during the forcible feeding, and on one occasion struck her in the face."

MRS. ROY ROTHWELL, who suffered imprisonment, stated with respect to the treatment of Suffragist prisoners : "None but vindictive and self-seeking officials can fail to admit that the Suffragists are political offenders, and ought to be treated as such in prison . . . It is not only injuring their bodies, but violating their honour and personal privacy ; it is to treat them like animals. To be dragged by force, frog-marched to the feeding-chair, bound in a sheet and held down by wardresses, while a tube is thrust up the nostrils by one doctor and food poured down by another, is to be outraged in every part of one's nature, and is calculated to drive one insane, as it did in the case of Mr. Ball."

DR. FRANCES EDE, of 13, Upper Berkeley Street, Portman Square, who was released from Aylesbury Prison on Thursday, April 11, 1912, in a letter to the "Standard," made the following statement : "Forcible feeding was instituted in most cases by the painful process of a tube through the nostrils. It so happened that I was one of the last to be forcibly fed by means of the nasal tube last Tuesday, and by far the more terrible experience than my personal suffering was to hear the agonising cries from other cells as the prisoners in turn were subjected to the painful treatment."

DR. ETHEL SMYTH, Mus. Doc., in a letter to the "Times," April 19, referring to the prison atrocities, says : "If, as Lord Rosebery tells us, the fundamental trait of the British character is a sense of fair play, one can count, once certain facts are known, on an outburst of surprise, indignation, and shame."

THE BLITZ

"Is the Canary alright?"

The most feared weapon at the outbreak of war was gas and the government of the day took the necessary precautions with thousands of cardboard coffins being ordered and mass graves prepared. As we now know massive gas attacks did not take place but the conventional bombing was continuous and on the worst night 1,792 people were injured and 1,436 killed. The bombing was indiscriminate, taking the life of an 11-hour-old baby and a woman who had spent one hundred years in the East End.

75. *All change!*

Many people dug their own shelters and others sought safety in the Underground stations, staying down for weeks on end. The stench was frightful with the sweat of unwashed humanity mixed with the smell of urine, excrement and strong carbolic. Many slept on the stairways; others were prevented from sleeping by the loud continuous snoring of their sleeping partners. Buckets were used when no toilets were available and it was often necessary to take the train to the next station to spend a penny. As might be imagined there was a serious increase in scabies, impetigo and lice though mercifully no epidemics.

The down-and-outs and vagrants had their own shelter near the Arches behind Charing Cross station. After years of drifting it was the start of a new life for some of them though others kept to their old ways. Over 15,000 lice were counted on one man's coat alone.

One of the largest and most famous shelters attracting sightseers from the West End was at Tilbury Railway arches in Stepney, housing up to 16,000 of the most deprived Londoners with children sleeping among sodden faeces and solid margerine.

Mickey's shelter was also on the 'black list' tour. This refuge was run in a democratic manner by Mickey Davis, an East End optician only 3'3" tall and hunch-backed. He oversaw one of the most overcrowded shelters with a steady stream of semi-conscious or unconscious people being passed towards the doorway.

Many Londoners for one reason or another would not leave their homes. In Mayfair the Sunday dinner was cooking in a public house, the landlord reading his newspaper whilst his wife was taking a bath on the top floor and the maid was between the two on the stairway, when the bomb dropped. The house was destroyed and the landlord killed outright, the maid slid down the bannisters, shaken and bruised but not seriously hurt. The bath from the top floor along with its occupant was thrown by the blast. The landlady was shocked and bruised and probably had difficulty finding the towel in the middle of the High Street.

The dinner still simmered on the stove.

A very different kind of stew was being tended a few miles further east. An old lady refused to stop stirring her supper even though the whole house around her had been blown away. To humour her a stretcher-bearer asked if he might taste her cooking and found that the pot was full of plaster and bricks.

Not all rescue workers were welcomed. One woman was found hanging by her hair from a hole in the ceiling; a well-meaning volunteer had to cut the womans pride and joy to set her free and was rewarded for his trouble with a slap in the face.

The most noted requests from old women being pulled from the rubble were 'Is the canary alright?' and 'Have you got a bottle of stout?' One girl was buried in Knightsbridge for forty-eight hours protected by a propped-up slab of concrete. She was later to say that her biggest discomfort was the air pollution caused by the dust. Her first request was for a cup of tea, her second . . . a cigarette.

The Café de Paris, which was advertised as being 'the safest nightclub in town' received a direct hit. The casualties were heavier than normal as the walls were covered with mirrors and the club packed with officers on leave. As one woman had her injured leg bathed with champagne, the looters set about their business.

Londoners had to look on the bright side of life and make light of their awful plight. A cartoon in one of the papers showing a girl in a blacked-out train had the caption;

'Take your hand off my knee! . . . Not you! . . . You!'

76. Life goes on!

77. *Several of the gas masks were made in Germany.*

78. *German plane over the East End.*

79. *One of the many crowded shelters.*

80. London's burning!

81. Homeless but alive.

82. You didn't have far to go to catch the morning tube.

In a Kings Cross pub the landlord appointed a young man to help in the bar. He sacked him one month later after complaints from his customers that the beer was being watered down. The landlord explained his reasons for sacking the boy to his barman: 'First the draymen water it, then I water it, then you water it and now the lad is watering it. Obviously he is dishonest and will have to go'.

The criminal community were quick to exploit the mayhem and some of the articles found on the bombed corpses showed the darker side of life during The Blitz. One body was recovered with a jemmy strapped to the leg and forty car ignition keys were found in the pocket of another. There was no shortage of looters and murder did not stop just because there was a war on . . .

The most famous killer of this period was probably trapped because, like Jack the Ripper, he was left-handed. In 1942 a forty-two year old chemist was found in Marylebone, strangled with a red and green knitted scarf. Although the woman's clothes had been disarranged there was no evidence of rape and police at first thought it was a case of theft gone wrong. They did not know they were dealing with a cold-blooded psychopath. The only clue they had at the time was that because of the bruising they could determine that the killer was left-handed.

The police did not have long to wait for their next body to turn up as the very next day they were summoned to the scene of a most sadistic crime. The body of a former Windmill girl was discovered naked in her Wardour Street flat. She was found spreadeagled with her throat cut and lower parts of her body savaged with a tin opener, which lay nearby and the wounds were such that it seemed the murderer was trying to open a can. The fingerprints from the opener proved to come from a left-handed person; this was more than coincidence.

Three days later another body was found and we can only hope that the woman was dead from strangulation before the other attacks took place on her as her sexual organs had been mutilated with a bread knife, two kitchen knives, a thin iron poker and a candle. Fingerprints from empty glasses showed the presence of a left-handed man.

The fourth victim in four days was discovered a few hours later. Although there were no fingerprints the 40 year old slim blonde had been butchered in a similar way to the previous two victims though this time with a razor.

Meanwhile across London the headmaster's son with his wavy hair and good looks had teased another young lady into a goodnight kiss. The twenty-eight-year old was very attractive to women in his RAF uniform and she was certainly not the first girl to fall for his charms. He put his hand up to her face as if to hold it during the embrace and the next thing the young girl knew was that she was being strangled. She managed to cry out and the airman fled as would-be rescuers came to her aid. He had however made

his first mistake. Aircraftman Gordon Frederick Cummins had rushed from the scene to an air-raid shelter but in his haste had left behind his respirator with his name and address. The married man was easily traced and after analysing fingerprints the police found some of the murdered women's goods in his possession.

Cummins denied all the charges but it took the jury only thirty-five minutes to find him guilty and despite appeals, he was hanged during an air-raid, on June 25th, 1942.

Murder was not the only crime perpetrated during the war years. There was also a prosecution under the 1735 Witchcraft Act with Helen Duncan being sentenced to nine months imprisonment after a most spectacular trial involving the most famous mediums of the day.

As the bombing intensified many children were sent to live in the country. It was a real education for both the city children and their substitute parents with H.G. Wells commenting:

'Parasites and skin diseases, vicious habits and insanitary practices have been spread, as if in a passion of egalitarian propaganda from the slums of such centres as Glasgow, London and Liverpool throughout the length and breadth of the land.'

Some of the country people were shocked at the appearance and behaviour of the city kids. In London the children were used to having supper — a slice of bread and margerine — and eating it standing up. Nine out of ten children from Stepney had no bath of their own, one in twenty had no toilet training and one in six were lousy. Many of the evacuees were astonished to find a bed of their own as overcrowding in the capital had been rife and many were used to sleeping under the mattress.

One mother visiting her child in the country scolded her in the following manner;

'You dirty thing, messing up the middle of the lady's carpet . . . go and do it in the corner.'

The British have always been known for their fondness for animals and during The Blitz showed them as much care and attention as they did the children. Many of the dogs were evacuated, mainly to The Lake District for anything up to ten shillings per week, a truly large amount in those days. At the other end of the scale the cost of lodging a budgerigar was 1d per week.

Many owners did not want their pets to have to suffer during the war and approximately half a million dogs and cats (mostly cats) were destroyed in the first few days of the war. There were so many bodies that the RSPCA let it be known that they could not bury them quickly enough and over 80,000 were laid to rest in a secret mass burial ground in the East End.

Those owners who could not bear to be parted from their pets bought gas-proof kennels and gas masks for their dogs. Ironically many of these were made in Germany.

The dogs and cats soon adapted to the new regime and often heard the sirens before their owners. Several of the animals were also able to differentiate between the warning and all-clear and there are several stories of human lives being saved by the alertness of their pets.

Food for the animals was rather scarce and horse-meat intended for the pet population was deliberately stained. It is very likely that many of the steaks bought on the black market and sold to unsuspecting customers was the same horse-meat. Food was becoming so scarce that it became an offence to feed bread to the birds. In 1942 the German U-boat campaign was having such an effect that the canning of dogs was seriously considered.

Any stray bombs hitting London Zoo might have resulted in lions and tigers running through the streets of London to add to the general mayhem so many animals were evacuated to Whipsnade and the aquarium drained. Much to the dismay of the zoo-keepers the venomous snakes and spiders had to be put to death.

Residents of Regents Park could hardly believe their eyes after one bombing as a frightened zebra made its way down the main street. They might also have noticed a colony of rhesus monkeys in the trees of their back gardens. The animals evaded capture for several days.

There were very few visitors to the zoo and those that went felt it was more a case of their being watched by the animals. One woman who visited with a precious and rare bag of peanuts became very popular.

83. 'And the little one said.'

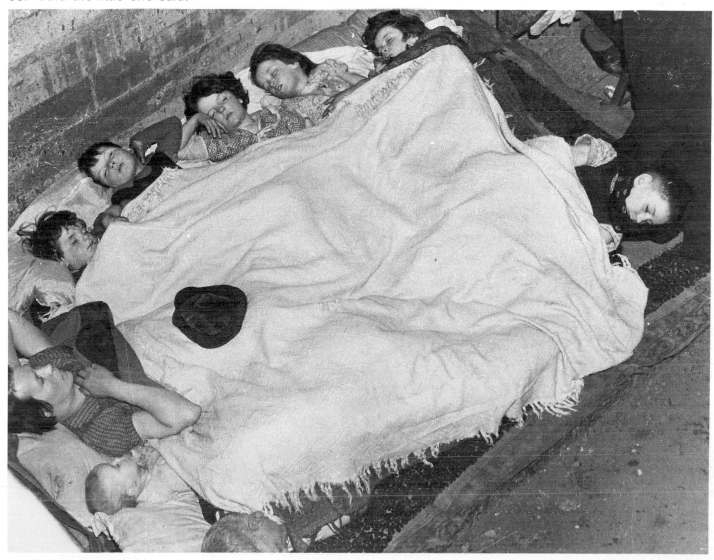

ACKNOWLEDGEMENTS

Writing a second book is certainly easier than writing the first though no less enjoyable. Few writers can work entirely alone and I am indebted to several friends for their expertise.

Joan went through the text with 'a fine toothcomb' pointing out errors and correcting clumsy sentences. Derek and the beast from Retford helped with artwork and layout advice and once again Elaine of Tragical History Tours transferred the manuscript to our computer.

My main thanks must go to the celebrated artist in burnt clay — John Clayton. We both fell in love with Edith Thompson's photograph and spent several enjoyable evenings in Nottingham's hosteleries drinking Shipstone's bitter and discussing the contents of the book. He was always honest and positive in his advice. I would like to thank my brother Terry in advance as his is the job of selling and delivering. Finally, I would like to thank all those who wrote complimentary letters about the first book. These were very much appreciated.

ILLUSTRATION ACKNOWLEDGEMENTS

Many thanks are given to the following for permission to reproduce their pictures:

Hulton Picture Library: 1, 2, 3, 4, 5, 6, 7, 10, 12, 13, 14, 38, 39, 46, 49, 50, 69, 73.

Syndication International: 9, 11, 15, 16, 19, 20, 21, 22, 23, 24, 25, 26, 27, 28, 29.

Mary Evans Picture Library: 40, 41, 42, 43, 44, 45, 53, 54, 55, 68, 74.

Tower Hamlets Library: 47, 48, 59, 61, 62, 64, 65.

The Imperial War Museum: 75, 76, 77, 78, 79, 80, 81, 82, 83.

The Museum of London: 70, 71, 72.

Madame Tussauds: 8, 17, 18.

Stevenage Library: 51, 52.

Gordon Fraser Cards: 56, 58.

All other illustrations from the author's collection.

THE AUTHOR

Steve Jones's wicked history.

CAPITAL OFFENCES: One parking ticket, 1972.

MURDER 'ORRIBLE MURDER: Arsenal vs Charlton Athletic — any season.

LEISURE: Steve may be found at every Charlton Athletic football match.

FOOD AND DRINK: Indian food and Shipstone's beer.

EDUCATION: Steve Jones is a peripatetic teacher of Modern Languages in Nottinghamshire.

HEALTH: Good, touch wood.

TRANSPORTATION: Renault Extra Van and bike.

MURDER: On his mind most days since May 3rd, 1979.

SEX: Steve Jones is male.

Tragical History Tours Ltd.

PRESENT

TRIP TO MURDER

A unique three hour evening bus trip combining cultural with criminal history with horror. Jack the Ripper, a haunted house, Greenwich, Tower, two pub stops, live commentary.

EVERY EVENING EXCEPT SATURDAY
MEET BUS OUTSIDE TEMPLE UNDERGROUND 7.00 p.m.

THE GHOST BUS

A lantern-lit trip through the haunted and chilling Chislehurst Caves.

MEET BUS
EMBANKMENT
UNDERGROUND
7.00 p.m. SUNDAYS

THE LONDON OF SHERLOCK HOLMES

Visit the scenes of crime solved by the capital's most celebrated detective.

MEET BUS TEMPLE
UNDERGROUND EVERY
SATURDAY, TUESDAY 7.00 p.m.

Reservations for all trips Tel: 857 1545.
Prices: All tours — Adults £10.50; Children £7.50.
Live expert commentary on all tours.